William Y. Adams

Culture
&
Thought

a psychological
introduction

Cross-cultural research is like virtue—everybody is in favor of it, but there are widely differing views of what it is and ought to be.

N. Frijda and G. Jahoda

Culture
&
Thought

a psychological
introduction

Michael Cole & Sylvia Scribner

The Rockefeller University

John Wiley & Sons, Inc.

New York London Sydney Toronto

Library of Congress Cataloging in Publication Data
Cole, Michael, 1938-
  Culture and thought: a psychological introduction.

  Includes bibliographical references.
  1. Cognition. 2. Personality and culture.
I. Scribner, Sylvia, 1923- joint author.
II. Title. [DNLM: 1. Cognition. 2. Cross-cultural
comparison. 3. Culture. BF311 C689p 1974]
BF311.C558   155.9′2   73-16360
ISBN 0-471-16478-X
ISBN 0-471-16477-1 (pbk.)

Printed in the United States of America

10 9 8 7 6 5 4 3 2 1

preface

Many years ago, at a conference on culture and cognition, Roger Brown observed that when graduate students were asked what they planned to study upon completion of their dissertations, a favorite response was that they would like to study how "someone else" (children, or cats, or some primitive peoples) would perform in the same task they had just labored over with college students. So it has been with cross-cultural research; curiosity about human variability, and often as not fortuitous location in an exotic setting, have provided the impetus for an ever-increasing number of studies, books, and specialized journals.

It was chance that brought each of us, separately, to research on culture and cognition. Yet each of us, in a continuing effort to broaden and deepen our understanding of the human mind, has been motivated to seek order in the chaotic flow of scholarly work that besets us.

This small book is intended to fulfill two purposes. We would like to introduce the beginning student to the variety of fascinating questions, phenomena, and theories that form the core of our understanding of culture and cognition. We also hope to influence the advanced student and professional who have, with good reason, looked with suspicion on the work that we discuss here. It is our belief that the proper use of comparative research designs can make a unique contribution to the study of human thought. This tool has been misused and poorly understood. In the chapters that follow we present some new approaches to the study of cultural influences on cognition. We hope that these formulations can serve as a basis for proper use and understanding of cross-cultural, psychological research.

New York 1973

Michael Cole
Sylvia Scribner

contents

Culture

&

Thought

a psychological
introduction

chapter 1 *Introductory Observations*

This book is concerned with a very old and very general problem: Are the cognitive processes of people reared in different cultural settings different? And if so, how do they differ? Partly because of its generality, partly because of long-standing confusions about the nature of *culture* and *cognition*, and partly because of special problems involved in drawing inferences from data acquired on many levels of observation, no clearly adequate answer to this question exists at the present time.

It will be the purpose of this book to examine the roots of the difficulties encountered in attempts to answer the question: Are there cultural differences in cognitive processes? We will begin with an historical account of various scholarly approaches to this question. Our major emphasis, however, will be on a review and critical analysis of experimental studies carried out by psychologists in recent years. We hope not only to bring together some of the useful information that has been gathered, but to uncover ways in which our knowledge about culture and cognition can be extended and applied to contemporary social problems.

What Is Cognition?

The first difficulty we face is the great variety of ways that terms referring to cognition—terms like *thinking* and *perceiving*—are used in everyday speech and in many areas of scientific discourse. We might get psychologists to agree on some neutral definition of cognition as those processes by which man acquires, transforms, and uses information about the world. But in actual practice, different psychologists use the term to denote different kinds of human operations on information, depending on their point of view in psychology and the specific nature of their research. Yet differences among psychologists are minor compared to those existing among investigators of dissimilar intellectual backgrounds. Anthropologists and philologists, as well as psychologists, have studied the relation between culture and cognition extensively, and each of these disciplines has developed its own working definition of *thinking* or has come to use the term in a variety of specialized ways.

In order to make our discussion of these conceptual confusions concrete, let us consider some of the evidence that scholars have used to demonstrate the existence of cultural differences in cognitive processes.

1. The Kamayura Indians of Brazil do not make a distinction between blue and green; spots of either color are designated by a single word, meaning parrakeet colored (Werner, 1961, p. 284). This is taken as evidence that these people manifest a "diffuse conceptual construction" with respect to color concepts.

2. It has been observed in Western-style administrative courts in South Africa that native witnesses, when asked to account for some event, begin their accounts with some other event greatly preceding the critical event in time. For instance, if asked to tell about an accident that occurred at 5:00 P.M., the witness might begin his account by relating all of his experiences from the time he arose in the morning. Such observations led Bartlett (1932) to hypothesize that these natives had learned a particular way of remembering that required them to start at the beginning of any sequence in order to remember one of its later elements. This remembering process was said to be different from that of the ordinary Englishman.

3. In central Liberia, as well as many other parts of Africa, it is believed that certain men (variously called *zos, shamen,* and *witchdoctors*) can control lightning and direct it to hit anyone or anything they choose. As evidence of such powers, a college student from this region offered the following story: In his town there was an occasion upon which someone stole meat from the cooking pot of the lightning *zo.* Angered, the *zo* announced that if the meat was not returned immediately, he would direct lightning to hit the guilty person on the following Saturday. On the appointed day, the meat had not been returned and the people all took to their houses in fear; a storm blew up, and when it was over the people found a dead dog, apparently killed by lightning. The student, and all the townspeople, took the dog's death as *prima facie* evidence of the power of the *zo.*

4. Referring to a preliterate epic poet, Havelock (1963) has said "We can be misled by some of . . . [his] vocabulary into thinking that he can manage an abstraction. We draw this conclusion however only if we ignore syntactical context and concentrate on the word itself which is an improper method of evaluating its effect on the consciousness of the audience" (pp. 188–189).

The first example raises several important issues. Do the Kamayura Indians *see* colors differently from the way we do? Or is it merely that their language differs from ours in the way in which it labels parts of the color spectrum? Can we infer differences in the perceptual processes of people in two cultures from differences in their color vocabularies? Still further, can we make judgments about mental categories (concepts) on the basis of language categories, as Werner attempts to do in the quoted passage? Clearly this passage touches off many complex questions involving the relation of language to perception and thought, as well as the validity of using linguistic evidence to make inferences about perception and thought.

The example of African memory habits raises different questions and suggests several alternative interpretations. Perhaps a difference in memory processes is not involved. Perhaps all that is involved in the court case is a difference in the witness's interpretation of what he is supposed to do. The witness may consider events prior to that in question as important. Or he may be trying to indicate his lack of involvement by talking about side issues. These ambiguities cannot easily be resolved unless we move from the plane of observation to that of experimentation, setting up special situations in which the subject's memory habits can be investigated free of such doubts. But creating a special experimental situation does not end our difficulties; it simply provides a new set. How representative is our experimental task? To what extent is it legitimate to argue from a single performance, or even a restricted set of performances, to performance-in-general within the culture? If our real interest is in the cognitive processes underlying performance, do we not require a representative set of performances from which to draw inferences?

The example of a belief in lightning magic illustrates still other ambiguities in the use of terms. Consider the different senses of the word *thinking* that might seem to apply to this example. If we were to try to compare our thinking about lightning magic with that of Liberians, we might say, "We don't think that a *zo* can direct lightning." In this statement, *think* is used in the general sense of *believe*. We are comparing our beliefs about human capabilities and weather phenomena with Liberian beliefs. We might also say after listening to the story, "We don't think that the *zo* made the lightning hit the dog," meaning that we do not conclude from what was told us that this event occurred—we are unconvinced by the evidence. Here *think* is used to refer to our evaluation of the relation between evidence and its implications. It is one thing to say that Liberians and American college students have different belief systems and may consequently make use of different evidence. It is another to say that the processes by which Liberians draw conclusions from evidence differ from ours, that we *reason* differently. This example indicates that we are going to have to be very careful to specify what we mean by *thinking* when we try to discuss data relevant to the question of culture and thinking, because our conclusions may very well depend upon our definitions: Are we referring to beliefs or processes? Is the question of logic relevant? Can one make inferences about logical processes from evidence about beliefs?

The final example is included because it raises some of the same issues as the other examples, with the additional feature that the person being discussed is one whose writings are read by almost every college student. Havelock is referring to Homer, the Greek epic poet. Homer's poems are among the great classics of world literature, yet his thought processes are said to differ fundamentally from ours. Homer, it is claimed, lacked the capacity for abstract thinking—an assertion commonly made about the thinking of people in nonindustrialized societies. Here we encounter another theme dominating many discussions of culture and cognition: the idea that our thinking is not only reflected in the language we speak but is limited by that language. This idea is generally supported by citing evidence of *concreteness* or *abstraction* in the vocabulary and grammar of a language. Is there such a thing as a concrete or abstract language, and if so, what is its relation to abstract and concrete thought?

These are some of the questions that we want to bring to bear on the material amassed by anthropologists and psychologists. We are interested in finding out what has been learned about *how* people perceive the environment, *how* they classify it, *how* they think about it. Our concern, therefore, will always be to get beneath the performance shown in a particular situation to the psychological processes responsible for it. This will require us to scrutinize carefully the nature of the experimental task used by the investigator so that we have some idea of what kind of a performance we are dealing with, and to respect the ambiguities involved in drawing valid inferences from data.

What Is Culture?

If investigators have difficulty with the psychological concept of cognition, there is unhappily little less confusion over the anthropological concept of culture.

It might appear at first blush that there should be no problem in knowing that the people you are studying are members of a different culture, and in most cases this has been true. When Margaret Mead went off to live with the Manus people of New Guinea, she knew that she was observing Manus culture. The definitional problem arises when you ask the question: What features of Manus life make us aware that there is such a thing as Manus culture? Some seem obvious at first: the people all speak a particular language called Manus; they dress in a noticeably different way from Americans; they build their houses in a common and (to us) unusual way; they share common beliefs about the world and treat their children in a distinctive fashion. There is simply no question about it, they are Manus!

But which of these things are necessary to define *culture*? For example, we can speak of both a Spanish culture and a Peruvian culture even though a vast majority of people in both groups speak the same language. We can speak of European culture in spite of large variations in dress, language, child-rearing practices, and religious beliefs among the people on the continent.

These kinds of considerations have led many scholars to deemphasize the quest for a universally acceptable definition of "what culture really is." Instead attention is drawn to some range of social phenomena that appears important for the purpose at hand. E. B. Tylor (1871), for example, felt that the anthropologist's job was like that of a naturalist: his business was to classify details of culture "with a view to making out their distribution in geography and history and the relations which exist among them." This aim is reflected in his famous definition that treats culture as an inventory of discrete, equally important phenomena or, in his words, a complex "which includes knowledge, belief, art, morals, law, custom and any other capabilities and habits acquired by man as a member of society" (1871, p. 1).

Tylor's contemporary, Lewis Morgan, was interested in another enterprise. To Morgan, the challenging problem in culture study was to trace the progression of human society from one stage of organization to the next, each characterized by an increase in man's conscious control of nature. Thus he selected for emphasis certain aspects of social life that most clearly revealed the principle stages of human development. These included the arts of subsistence, which he felt provided the motor force of cultural advance, and primary institutions such as government, the family, and property. His major work, *Ancient Society* (1877), deals with the origin and development of these factors, leaving untouched other features of culture dealt with by Tylor. Concerned with accounting for culture *change*, Morgan nowhere defines (in *Ancient Society*) what culture *is*.

These different anthropological definitions of culture illustrate the difficulties investigators encounter when they try to relate phenomena on a cultural level to those on an individual psychological level. Which particular aspects of culture should be singled out as potentially important from the causal point of view? Some guiding hypotheses are clearly essential if investigations are not to proceed on a hit-and-miss basis. But as yet there is no general theory or conceptual framework in psychology that would generate specific hypotheses about how culturally patterned experiences influence the development of cognitive processes in the individual.

In the absence of such guidelines, psychologists in the early period of cross-cultural work depended on obvious distinctions between populations (say aborigines and Englishmen) to sustain their comparative studies. Global comparisons of this kind, however, proved singularly unenlightening. If almost everything about the way of life of two groups is different, what can we learn about causation by demonstrating a difference in performance on a single task?

This tendency to compare cultures as though they were homogeneous units that could be lined up against each other has diminished in recent years. Investigators have singled out a certain few sociocultural factors as potential causal mechanisms for specific phenomena. Among these have been language, urbanization, formal educational institutions, and literacy. In addition, ecological features such as the nature of the landscape (jungle versus artic expanse) and economic factors such as subsistence activities (hunting versus planting) have figured in psychological explanations. While this search for factors that can make a difference *within* cultures as well as *between* cultures is certainly an advance, it still has serious drawbacks. For one thing, it suggests rather simple connections between culture and cognition; in reality, cultural features rarely operate in isolation. For example, many anthropologists have speculated that literacy is a crucial factor in changing the way people think. But, except in rare cases, literacy co-occurs with other cultural features such as the presence of formal education, increased industrialization, and urbanization. When we find, as many have, that educated and uneducated rural Africans differ in their performance of some cognitive task, how are we to say what features of their cultures caused the difference? Furthermore, simply showing a relation between some aspect of culture and some aspect of individual performance does not tell us anything about the nature of the connection between them; yet that is precisely the psychologist's interest.

One final word about some of the conceptual difficulties in this field. When we talk about a relation between culture and cognition, it might appear that we are dealing with two separate sets of phenomena that make contact with each other under special circumstances, which it is the scientist's task to discover (something like two billiard balls colliding on a pool table). But just as it is fanciful to conceive of man existing outside of social life, we cannot imagine any intellectual function that does not have a sociocultural character. Perception, memory, and thinking all develop as part of the general socialization of a child and are inseparably bound up with the patterns of activity, communication, and social relations into which he enters. The very physical environment that he encounters has been transformed by human effort. His every experience has been shaped by the culture of which he is a member and is infused with socially defined meanings and emotions. Consider language, for example. It is at one and the same time a vital social force and an individual tool of communication and thought; it is, so to speak, on both sides of the culture-cognition relationship.

How can we handle these complexities? What this book will try to demonstrate is that we can not hope to escape from these complexities by setting up, as a criterion, a hypothetical individual with cognitive capacities that are free from the influences of culture. The "isolated individual" is a myth. Nor can we hope to measure cognitive capacities by means of some idealized test that is itself culture-free. We would delude ourselves if we thought such a test were possible. Instead we have to discover a strategy of research that will help us uncover how individual and cultural processes interweave with each other as the child develops and becomes integrated into society. And that is the subject matter of this book.

Summary

It should be clear from this brief discussion that the study of culture and cognition is a very diffuse enterprise. The idea of employing variations in cultural experience to decide basic questions about the nature of human nature is very attractive. But scholars have failed to arrive at any general consensus about how to proceed. Instead we have a situation in which each investigator starts from his own basic assumptions and proceeds by means of his own data-gathering techniques. The range of phenomena and the variety of explanations that a hundred years of such uncoordinated scholarly activity has produced are immense. They cover not only the multitude of theories and experimental situations that are common to the broad field of cognitive psychology, but problems of anthropology and linguistics as well.

In the light of this diversity, complete coverage of the "facts" about culture and cognition is not only a difficult undertaking, but one likely to be incoherent and unenlightening. Within certain very prescribed areas experiments have led to reasonable and useful generalizations. As a rule, however, investigators have not pursued any single line of work long enough to bring the issues at stake to a clear resolution. Consequently, it is necessary to patch together evidence from an often-bewildering array of cultures and techniques in order to illuminate any specific culture–cognition relation (as, for example, the relation between literacy and memory). This makes both the writers' job of exposition and the readers' job of interpretation quite difficult. It will often seem, in the chapters to follow, that the experiments reviewed are totally unrelated, like multicolored chips in a kaleidoscope. This situation should be recognized for what it is, a deficiency characteristic of current scholarship, and not a deficiency in the reader's conceptual capacities.

The material we have selected for discussion does, however, represent some rules of selection. While we will refer from time to time to other fields of research, our main emphasis will be primarily *experimental* in nature, not purely out of methodological bias but because there has been little psychological work on cognitive processes employing observational or quasi-experimental methods. Our survey is by no means complete, nor is it intended to be; its purpose is to provide the reader with a grasp of major questions and investigative techniques.

In an attempt to bring some order out of chaos, we have organized the chapters that follow according to relatively traditional categories currently used in cognitive psychology. At the end of each chapter, we provide a summary of the work within that particular problem area. In the final chapter we return to the broader issues raised here and attempt to integrate concepts and phenomena that have customarily been dealt with on an isolated basis.

chapter 2 *A Brief History*

Much of the history of research on culture and cognition has been dominated by the controversy between those who maintain that there are no fundamental differences in human thinking across cultures and others who insist that such differences are critical to an understanding of man's nature.

More recently, these sweeping generalities about universal characteristics of man have tended to be replaced by questions concerning how specific cultural differences might be related to specific cognitive differences. It is useful, however, to review the principal positions in the earlier controversies and to evaluate the evidence and procedures upon which they rested. Examining classic theories can help us understand some of the lines of investigation now pursued in cross-cultural studies. While many current studies disavow theoretical frameworks and seem to focus on specialized issues, their assumptions often show continuity with earlier approaches.

Reexamining these approaches in the light of contemporary research may suggest new

11

and more valuable ways of raising questions about the relation between culture and cognition.

But this is by no means an easy task. So great has been the intellectual challenge posed by these questions that scholars and scientists from many disciplines have attempted to grapple with them. Over the centuries, sociologists, anthropologists, philosophers, linguists, and psychologists have all put forward theories linking culture and mind. These theories have been in the grand tradition and deal with fundamental philosophic and scientific concepts. In a brief review, we cannot begin to deal adequately with this theoretical spectrum nor, for that matter, with any one of the major controversies that have developed within it. What we hope to do is give the reader a glimpse of this area from the heights—in its broadest and most panoramic perspective—and to introduce the great thinkers whose views still provide the silent framework within which most contemporary research takes place.

Cognitive Differences

The history of concern with cultural influences on thinking begins with an emphasis on differences.

It is not surprising that the adventurers and missionaries from western European societies of the sixteenth to eighteenth centuries should have been struck by the novel and unexpected characteristics of the life they encountered on new shores. Their observations and records featured aspects of behavior and social customs dramatically unlike those they knew at home. In their astounded discovery of the great diversity that characterizes humanity, they frequently overlooked those common aspects of social life that unify it (the existence of language, tools, family units, systems of morality and ideology, for example). Some even doubted that "those people" were "really human."

The voluminous records that travelers and colonial administrators left behind provided the basic source material for the new sciences that arose in the mid-nineteenth century. Scholars took their scientific problem to be one of accounting for the exotic facts reported in the informally accumulated ethnological literature. How could cultural differences be characterized and explained? Were they a consequence of innate differences among human groups, especially differences in mental faculties, or did human groups appear different only because their cultures were different?

This almost exclusive preoccupation with cultural differences was further reinforced by the dominant economic and political forces of the time. Contacts with nonindustrialized societies did not long remain sporadic and incidental. By 1850 England and other European nations had met and conquered traditional, non-technological societies on all the continents and had built extensive empires. Practical problems of administration called for the talents not only of military men and public officials, but of the new social scientists as well. Under such circumstances, concern with cultural differences all too often took the form of comparisons between "them" (the "uncivilized" in the colonies) and "us" (the "civilized" in the mother countries).*

Biological Accounts

One of the earliest and most influential theoretical schemes for relating mental and cultural phenomena was put forward by Herbert Spencer, a leading figure in English scientific and intellectual circles in the decades from 1850 to 1900. Spencer's life work was devoted to the construction of a *synthetic philosophy*, which he hoped would unify knowledge of the separate sciences. He thought that all the phenomena studied in the separate sciences could be explained by elementary laws of matter and motion. A number of years before the publication of Darwin's *Origin of Species*, Spencer had already begun to account for the history of all concrete things in the universe in terms of a single cosmic principle of evolution, which he thought regulated matter in motion.

According to Spencer, all things in the world—inorganic, organic, and superorganic—change over time in a definite direction. Simple forms that are initially homogeneous become more complex and heterogeneous. Their parts become increasingly differ-

---

*The terminology used in the works under review does not reflect modern usage, but for simplicity's sake we will retain the author's original terms in our exposition of their views. The reader should supply the quotation marks for such terms as "primitive," "uncivilized," "savage," and the like.

entiated; but at the same time they become better integrated and organized into superordinate and subordinate levels. The movement of evolution is from lower to higher, and more perfect, organization.

Shortly after Darwin demonstrated how evolutionary mechanisms operate in the biological world, Spencer attempted to show how the same principles regulated development in the psychological and social domains. He maintained that intellectual progress can be understood by the evolution of more-complex and more-general cognitions from simple cognitions and reflex actions, just as complex physical structures and functions evolve from simple ones. Similarly, society can be thought of as an organism, and its products—language, knowledge, material appliances, and arts—as becoming progressively more complex and highly organized (1888, Vol. 1).

While Spencer did not reduce psychological and social phenomena to biological phenomena, he resorted to biological mechanisms to account for their origin and the course of their development. He relied chiefly on the concepts of natural selection or survival of the fittest (which he credited Darwin with elaborating) and on the inheritance of acquired traits (the central tenet in the evolutionary theory of the biologist Lamarck). How did these concepts apply to mental phenomena? Spencer held that during the course of man's experience, he acquires certain mental traits that favor his continued existence and are passed down from generation to generation.

> The effects of the most uniform and frequent of these experiences have been successively bequeathed . . . and have slowly amounted to that high intelligence which lies latent in the brain of the infant —which the infant in after life exercises and perhaps strengthens or further complicates, and which with minute additions, it bequeathes to future generations. . . . Thus it happens that out of savages unable to count up to the number of their fingers and speaking a language containing only nouns and verbs, arise at length our Newtons and Shakespeares (Spencer, 1887, p. 471).

And what were Spencer's ideas about social evolution? Through the interplay between the nature of individuals in a social aggregate and external environmental forces (such as climate and plant life), societies develop more-varied and more-elaborate structures and products. Those people who more readily acquire higher physical and mental traits make the greatest social advances. Reciprocally, those who live in the most developed societies have experiences that further promote their intellectual faculties. Thus: "Development of the higher intellectual faculties has gone on *pari passu* with social advance, alike as cause and consequence" (Spencer, 1888, pp. 90–91).

As the mental traits and social environments of different peoples of the world diverge, the struggle for survival sets one group into conflict with another, by means of which the more powerful or "more adapted" drive "inferior varieties into undesirable habitats" and occasionally "exterminate them" (Spencer, 1888, p. 39). Since those who win are the more-adapted, Spencer's theory led to the conclusion that nineteenth-century Englishmen were of the highest mentality and lived in the most advanced society, representing a standard against which other people could be measured. Study of existing races at lower social levels, Spencer then argued, could show the mental traits that characterized early evolutionary forms of human life.

Two aspects of Spencer's analysis of the intellect of non-Western peoples are of special interest—his method of discovery, and his catalogue of mental traits. Spencer described his method of discovering evolutionary sequences as composed of two stages. First he deduced the leading traits of intellectual evolution from current psychological principles. Then he used the facts as described by travelers to demonstrate how the principles applied (1888, Vol. I). Although he brought an enormous amount of material to bear on this enterprise (over 2500 references in 455 works), almost all of it was unevaluated and anecdotal. Moreover, since this highly selective material was filtered through Spencer's theory of evolution, it is not too surprising that the facts that emerged as significant tended to fit the theory. As we shall see, this method continues to be employed as an investigative tool in the study of culture and cognition, even though some of its practitioners have conceptual frameworks quite different from Spencer's.

As for the mental traits Spencer enumerated, many of these, too, persist in the contemporary literature. Primitive thinking was said to exhibit the following "deficiencies," among others: no conception of general facts, no ability to anticipate future results, limited concepts, absence of abstract ideas, lack of idea of causality. On the other hand, the uncivilized have "acute senses and quick perceptions." They are imitative and "clever, rapid learners of simple ideas [but] incapable of taking in complex ideas. The primitive intellect develops rapidly and early reaches its limit" (Spencer, 1888).

Spencer's views were held in varying measure by the vast majority of scholars until the turn of the century. Within the general context of evolutionary theory, anthropologists and psychologists gave scientific respectability to a number of propositions promulgated by Spencer and popularly disseminated. One of these was the notion that primitives think like children. For example, E. B. Tylor, called by some the father of anthropology, viewed the imagination of nonliterate people as similar to that of European children. The observations that suggested this analogy were doll play in young children and a custom in some societies for mothers to carry around dolls of their dead children with the presumed purpose of warding off harmful spirits that might attack living children. Tylor states:

> The idol answers to the savage in one province of thought the same purpose that its analogue, the doll, does to the child. It enables him to give a definite existence and a personality to the vague ideas of higher beings, which his mind can hardly grasp without material aid (1865, p. 94).

One of the founders of developmental psychology in the United States, G. Stanley Hall, used a somewhat different theoretical framework to support this general line of thought. He was a strong supporter of the view that "ontogeny recapitulates phylogeny"—a famous aphorism by which was meant that the child's development goes through the same stages as the human race has traversed in its evolutionary development. This idea, taken over from biology, made it easy to accept the evidence concerning the "childlike" thought processes of primitive people as support for the general doctrine of *recapitulation*. Just as each child undergoes mental development, so does the race, the two processes being in fact the same. "Infancy, childhood and youth," said Hall, are from one point of view, "three bunches of keys to unlock the past history of the race" (1965, p. 47).

The flavor of this approach is contained in the following excerpt from the work of one of Hall's students.

> The mind of the child and the mind of the savage, when differences due to the presence of manhood and womanhood in the latter,

diversity of environment, influence of higher culture, prolonged infancy, social environment, etc., have been taken into consideration, present many interesting parallels of a general sort. *Naivete* that touches upon genius, suggestibility of great extent and sometimes of a very high order, resemblances in mental association, modes of thought and of thought-expression, dream-life, mind-content, initiation, conservatism, mythological ideas, personal and social ideas, sense-domination, love of analogy and symbolism, use and products of the imagination, love of nature and the world of plant and animal life, poetry and story-telling, myth-making, personification and other primal arts, language, art, music, etc. (Chamberlain, 1901, p. 456).

The prevailing biological orientation of the period was also expressed in the ubiquitous identification of cultural differences with racial differences. Spencer not only attributed lower mental traits to "inferior" races but to lower socioeconomic classes within the industrialized nations, who, he presumed, had taken their place in society by natural selection. While the identification of races varied enormously from one work to another, most nineteenth-century classifications shared with Spencer's the common feature of putting European society at the top of the evolutionary ladder (see Harris, 1968, Chap. 5). Tylor found it convenient to divide the human race by language families (Semitic, Aryan, and the like). While he held that stages of culture might be compared without taking into account "hereditary varieties of races," he was not averse to arranging the races on a rough scale of civilization. In doing this, he acknowledged that the "white invader or colonist . . . at best can hardly claim to substitute a life stronger, nobler, and purer at every point than that which he supersedes" (Tylor, 1871, p. 29), but he concluded nevertheless that "the general tenour of the evidence goes far to justify the view that on the whole the civilized man is not only wiser and more capable than the savage, but also better and happier" (1871, p. 31).

The anthropologist Marvin Harris has aptly characterized the historical role of doctrines of racial determinism in the social sciences. Observing that popular systems of prejudice are probably as old as humanity, he points out that the nascent social sciences put them on a new footing: "Prior to the 19th century, nations had never rewarded their wise men to prove that the supremacy of one people over another was the inevitable outcome of the biological laws of the universe" (Harris, 1968, p. 81).

About the turn of the century the climate of scientific theory began to change, and the racially based evolutionary theory of cognitive processes fell into disrepute. The biological hypothesis of the inheritance of acquired traits—on which Spencer placed great reliance for his entire theory of mental evolution—has become scientifically unacceptable with respect to the transmission of physical traits, let alone complex intellectual behaviors. No one today would seriously maintain that "mental peculiarities" caused by habit become organic and hereditary.

Moreover, the social sciences have amassed compelling evidence that the complex behavioral changes Spencer conceived of as biologically transmitted are acquired through experience and are culturally transmitted. A Chinese infant raised in France grows up to speak French, and the son of a tribal chief presumably genetically incapable of abstract reasoning attends English schools and becomes a Don at Oxford.

As for social evolution, the rapid changes in power relations among nations and in social groups within nations in this century make it difficult to resort to the slow processes of natural selection to account for social change. There is general agreement within the social sciences today that the principles that govern societal change are not the same as those that govern the development of species.

The classic attack on the identification of race with culture was made by Franz Boas in *The Mind of Primitive Man* more than fifty years ago. At the end of a long survey of the historical antecedents of modern societies, Boas reached the conclusion, ascribed to by the overwhelming majority of scholars, that there is no foundation for the equation of race and culture. Language families are independent of race as defined by any simple or single set of physical characteristics. Cultural forms differ among people classified as the same race (Peruvian Indians compared with northern Canadian Indians, for example). Moreover, history shows numerous examples of extensive changes in language and culture without corresponding changes in "blood." The two major examples cited by Boas are Europe in the Middle Ages and Japan in the modern era. Boas further illustrated the shifting, nonscientific nature of the race concept by reviewing various attempts at racial classification which have proceeded in the main by a hodgepodge of various and overlapping criteria—such as a mixture of geography and anatomy or of language and hair color (Boas, 1911).

Contemporary social and biological scientists have made even more thoroughgoing critiques of the position that genetically based racial differences account for cultural differences. While genetic specialties probably contributed to man's evolution from hominid to *homo sapiens* over the course of 2 million years, the modern consensus is that the rapid cultural advances of *homo sapiens* in its lifetime of approximately 50,000 years have little to do with genetic changes (see Harris, 1968). The overwhelming evidence that radical changes in culture can and do occur within the space of one generation without the possibility of genetic innovation makes it clear that the concept of *genetic transmission* is inapplicable as an explanation of cultural change.

Secondly, it has proved impossible to arrive at a scientific definition of subspecies within the human race and, accordingly, impossible to compare cognitive functioning or other behavioral characteristics along racial lines. (See Topoff, in press, for a lucid discussion of the status of the race concept). The persistence of the concept of race as a descriptive or explanatory construct despite failure to achieve a consensus on the defining attributes of races, suggests that the concept has a firmer sociological than biological base. As Herskovits pointed out in a recent reassessment of Boas's contribution, anthropological developments and world events in the last several decades have converged towards the conclusion that "the very concept of race [represents] a scientific dead-end" in the explanation of culture (Herskovits, 1965, p. 10).

A Sociological Account

The view that the thought processes of nonindustrial peoples are radically different from those of Europeans had another set of roots in addition to those found in evolutionary theory. This was the tradition of French sociology at the turn of the century, which, in the work of Comte, Durkheim, and others, stressed the critical role of the social collectivity in determining the characteristics and behavior of the individual. Lucien Levy-Bruhl, a friend of Durkheim, set out to analyze mental functioning from this point of view. Beginning in 1910, he published a series of monographs about primitive mentality; like Spencer, he relied exclusively on the published reports of missionaries, travelers, and early anthropological observers.

Levy-Bruhl maintained that the proper way to study individual mental functioning is through an analysis of the culture of which the individual is a member. He held that each culture may be characterized by a set of general beliefs, called "collective representations," which regulate the thought processes of the individuals in that group. The collective representations of the average European keep the intellectual, motor, and emotional realms distinct from each other. But the collective representations of primitives do not.

> Their [primitive] mental activity is too little differentiated for it to be possible to consider ideas or images of objects by themselves apart from the emotions which evoke those ideas or are evoked by them (1910, p. 23).

Levy-Bruhl claimed also that primitive mentality was "prelogical," by which he meant that "it does not bind itself down, as our thought does, to avoiding contradiction" (1910, p. 63).

These views met with strong and continuing disapproval from American scholars, among whom Boas was an early spokesman. In the same work in which he challenged racial interpretations of cultural differences, Boas attacked the evidence and methods used by Levy-Bruhl and others to "prove" differences in cognitive processes among cultural groups. First, he challenged the reliability of some of the ethnographic reports used as source material. As an example, one observer cited by both Spencer and Levy-Bruhl had concluded, on the basis of the fact that certain Indians quickly grew tired of conversation with him, that the "mind of the savage appears to rock to and fro out of mere weakness." But Boas had worked with the Indians in question and could testify that they generally manifested a lively interest in discussion and debate. If they failed to participate in the conversation, he claimed, it was probably because the traveler was boring them to death with trivia. In the same vein, would we be justified in concluding that college students have no capacity for abstract ideas because they doze off during a boring lecture?

Secondly, Boas challenged the whole idea that one can draw

inferences about thought processes from the traditional beliefs and customs of a people. He pointed out that were we to use traditional American beliefs about nature and society as evidence about logical processes, the conclusions would be as dismal as those drawn about natives' logic. This criticism has proved very important in the history of studies of culture and thinking because it invalidates the major source of data upon which scholars had previously rested their conclusions.

A further criticism of Levy-Bruhl made by contemporary anthropologists goes to the question, raised earlier in regard to Spencer's method, of the bias and selectivity involved in the culling of facts from the literature.

> It is in the use of sources that Levy-Bruhl is most vulnerable. Every anthropologist knows that one can construct almost any kind of theory and find cases to support it in the ethnographic literature. . . . Any theoretical statement remains a suggestive hypothesis until the dynamic connections have been documented by controlled research (Bunzel, 1966, p. xvi).

With few exceptions, psychologists also have been antagonistic to Levy-Bruhl's writings. Wolfgang Köhler, noted Gestalt psychologist, offered an alternative explanation for some of the phenomena Levy-Bruhl took as instances of mystical thinking. He illustrated in detail how certain dynamic principles of *perception* identified in Western cultures might account for so-called animistic beliefs in traditional cultures, making it unnecessary to hypothesize differences in *thought* processes. He went on to suggest that primitive perception might in fact be closer to reality than the modern view, in which people have learned to "see the world" through the eyeglasses of natural science (Köhler, 1961).

The English psychologist Sir Frederick Bartlett considered Levy-Bruhl's major fallacy to be his comparison of primitive thought with scientific thought. Bartlett maintained that if the ordinary members of both primitive and modern societies were compared, their mental functioning would reveal common characteristics.

> The error here, as in much recent social and abnormal psychology, is not that the primitive or the abnormal are wrongly observed, but that the modern and normal are hardly observed at all. . . . If we care to turn our attention to the practical inventiveness of primitive man in regard to the search for food, the provision of dwellings, and the development of material arts, it appears that he

is as capable of learning from experience as the most cultivated of our contemporaries. Moreover, within these realms he learns from experience in exactly the same ways as we do (Bartlett, 1923, pp. 284–285).

Psychological Accounts

The work of the developmental psychologist Heinz Werner contains a characterization of non-Western thought with echos of Spencer and Levy-Bruhl (Werner, 1957; see also Werner and Kaplan, 1956, and Werner, 1961). Werner shares with the early evolutionary theorists an interest in *changes* that occur in mental functioning across species and within the human species. He finds such changes to be orderly and directional, as they did; but he does not seek to account for them by biological mechanisms, nor does he use social phenomena, such as Levy-Bruhl's collective representations, for explanatory purposes. Rather, he appeals to the general concept of development, which "rests on one basic assumption, namely that wherever there is life, there is growth and development, that is, formation in terms of systematic orderly sequence" (Werner, 1957, p. 125). The developmental approach has been useful in systematizing biological phenomena in various fields, he states, and can similarly "coordinate within a single framework forms of behavior observed in comparative animal psychology, in child psychology, in psychopathology, in ethnopsychology, and in the general and differential psychology of man in our own culture" (1957, p. 125).

Development in all these forms of life is, according to Werner, regulated by the *orthogenetic principle*—wherever development occurs, it proceeds from a state of relative lack of differentiation to a state of increasing differentiation, articulation, and hierarchic integration (Werner and Kaplan, 1956). (Compare Spencer's formulation of the course of evolution on p. 13). Werner is careful to point out that, unlike G. Stanley Hall and other recapitulationists, he does not treat developmental sequences in animals, children, and cultures as *materially identical* but only as similar or parallel. Nonetheless, when he uses the term *primitive mental activities*, he refers to forms of thought that are presumably present in certain animals, in children in Western cultures, in adults as well as children in non-Western cultures, and in Western mental patients who have regressed to earlier levels of development.

According to Werner, nonliterate people, children, and mental patients all manifest primitive thinking in such spheres as the following: failure to differentiate between subject and object (as not knowing the difference "between what one dreams and what one sees"); use of concrete modes of classification; failure to separate thought processes from perceptions, emotions, and motor actions, and thus failure to achieve an abstract mode of thought. While Werner draws on experimental findings, including his own experimental work, for his conclusions in respect to animals, children, and psychopaths, his generalizations concerning primitive man rely on pretty much the same material and procedures used by Levy-Bruhl. His comparative approach is illustrated in the following excerpts from *Comparative Psychology of Mental Development* (1961):

> It appears that grouping on the basis of perceptual configuration is reflected in the classificatory phenomena of *primitive languages* [italicized in the original]. One peculiarity of these languages is that the verbal classification of several single objects by means of one name common to all is not always dependent on any actual common likeness (p. 225).

> This primitive type of classification based on a togetherness of different things in a realistic situation can be clearly observed in the early ontogenetic stages of *child language*. Lombroso reports one child who designated both duck and water by "qua-qua." Another used "afta" to mean drinking-glass, pane of glass, windows and also what was drunk out of the glass (p. 226).

> It is especially instructive to observe that a concrete naturalistic grouping appears in the *pathologically* regressed mentality. A catatonic woman created a language that exhibits a most extraordinary method of word construction. She completed a whole dictionary of normal terms translated into her own private language. Instead of the word "thistle," for example, she used "le stone" (with the French article). The verbal identification of "thistle" and "stone" depends on the fact that they both belong to the same (affectively conditioned) collective situation and are therefore interchangeable (p. 228).

Werner's views have led to little cross-cultural research, but some recent findings, especially in the areas of perception and classification reviewed in later chapters, are helpful in evaluating it.

A general problem with Werner's orthogenetic principle is that it *describes* developmental levels of organization but suggests no mechanisms by which development proceeds from one level to another. The notion that development is a natural genetic process cannot elucidate the specific relation between cultural experience and cognition. Why should one level be reached in one culture and not in others?

Jerome Bruner, an American psychologist well known for his studies of perceptual and cognitive processes, has applied himself to this question and has attempted to work out a theory linking particular aspects of culture to cognitive growth. Intelligence, according to Bruner, is to a great extent the internalization of "tools" provided by a given culture, including not only technological hardware but symbolic systems as well. Cultures may differ in their repertoire of tools and in the social institutions that they develop for the transmission of knowledge and tool-using skills. Among institutions having the greatest impact on cognitive growth is the Western-type school, which structures learning experiences in a unique way. In school, learning is separated from everyday practical activities, language is used out of context for special analytic purposes, and the new tool of written language is made available for cognitive operations. School learning thus demands, and fosters, abstract modes of thought.

Unlike others whose work has been discussed so far, Bruner has based his theorizing on data gathered from psychological experimentation in other cultures rather than on surveys of the anthropological literature. In a study conducted among the Wolof tribe in Senegal, West Africa (reviewed in Chapter 6), the performance of Wolof schoolchildren on a concept-formation task was more like that of middle-class schoolchildren in Boston than like their unschooled neighbors. This and other findings led Bruner to conclude that if school-type intellectual training is not forthcoming,

> then one finds forms of intellectual functioning that are adequate for concrete tasks but not so for matters involving abstract conception. . . . In short, some environments "push" cognitive growth better, earlier and longer than others. What does not seem to happen is that different cultures produce completely divergent and unrelated modes of thought. The reason for this must be the constraint of our biological heritage. That heritage makes it possible for man to reach a form of intellectual maturity that is capable of elaborating a highly technical society. Less demanding societies—less demanding intellectually—do not produce so much symbolic embed-

ding and elaboration of first ways of looking and thinking. Whether one wishes to "judge" these differences on some universal human scale as favoring an intellectually more evolved man is a matter of one's values (Greenfield and Bruner, 1969, p. 654).

This contemporary view of cognitive differences is a long way from the earlier anthropological contrasts between two kinds of mentality, which were described as bipolar opposites—all the essential aspects of the one presumably missing from the other. In Bruner's view, whatever cognitive differences may exist among people of different cultures are limited by the constraints of a common heritage and many shared features of mental life.

Cognitive Universals

Anthropological Views

Given the massive evidence that there are differences in mental functioning among cultural groups, the idea that there are no substantial cultural differences in thought *processes* may not seem worthy of examination. But several contemporary social science theorists take just this point of view. Like Boas, they argue that the "functions of the human mind are common to the whole of humanity" (Boas, 1965, p. 135). Whereas earlier social scientists took observed differences among cultures as *prima facie* evidence of underlying cognitive differences, these contemporary approaches consider the observed cultural dissimilarities to be merely different manifestations of common underlying cognitive structures.

Typical is the following statement by an anthropologist on this point:

> The reasoning and thinking processes of different peoples in different cultures do not differ . . . just their values, beliefs and ways of classifying differ (quoted in Cole and Gay, 1972, p. 1066).

According to this view, observed differences are in the area of *content*: the belief systems and cultural premises of traditional people may differ from those in industrialized societies, but they embody the same logical processes and concern with relation of cause and effect. Similarly, classifications or concepts may differ in terms of what objects and phenomena are grouped together and what attributes are used for grouping, but all classifications are arrived at by the same processes of abstraction and generalization.

Just as evolutionary theory played a significant role in the development of theories of human differences, a contemporary philosophical and methodological approach in the sciences and humanities—*structuralism*—has strongly contributed to the search for common principles underlying human cultural diversity.

The essential aspects of the structural approach can be illustrated by the work of Claude Levi-Strauss, a distinguished French anthropologist (1963, 1966).

Levi-Strauss explicitly repudiates the concept that there are lower and higher levels of mental development. On the contrary, he maintains that there are no differences in how the mind works from one culture to another or from one historical epoch to another. Primitive and Western scientific thought systems simply represent different strategies by which man makes nature accessible to rational inquiry. Both strategies seek objective knowledge of the universe; both proceed by ordering, classifying, and systemizing information; both create coherent systems. What then are the differences? According to Levi-Strauss, the basic difference is in the *material* used for thought—for example, the kinds of attributes that are used in forming classes. Primitive classification systems are based on qualities that are readily seen and experienced, whereas modern science relies more on properties that are inferred from necessary relations in the structure of the objects classified. For example, fruits and vegetables are classified by the average shopper in ways quite different from those of the botanist. Primitive classification systems generalize from the tangible properties of the members of the system and are thus limited by the concrete experience of the community.

Levi-Strauss suggests that there is an intimate relation between modes of classifying objects and ways of solving problems. Primitive science is exemplified by the *bricoleur*, or jack-of-all-trades, who has a fixed bag of things that he uses to make other things. The tools are never specifically designed for the task at hand, but rather constitute a collection of things preserved because they might come in handy. Their function depends upon the particular occasion in which they are used. The jack-of-all-trades is contrasted with the engineer, whose inventory of tools is variable, its composition depending on the task at hand. At the same time, the objects making up the engineer's inventory have fixed and stable purposes, whereas in the primitive's system a particular object is likely to have an amorphous and shifting status.

Levi-Strauss's generalizations are based on his analyses of classification systems, myths, kinship structures, and other cultural institutions and products. While he views his enterprise as one that demonstrates the universal and unconscious activities of the human mind, he is not directly studying psychological processes in the individual. His principal significance for the study of culture and cognition is his demonstration that ethnological material embodying the endlessly varied products of many cultures still testifies to common underlying human operations.

Linguistic Approaches

Additional support for cognitive universals comes from new developments in the science of language. These emphasize the complexity of all language systems; they deny that languages can be arranged on a scale of simplicity or complexity, or that conclusions about the cognitive structures of language users can be derived from a comparative analysis of language vocabularies. Modern linguists tend to stress the importance of *structural* features of language that are shared by all languages. They point out, for example, that all languages are composed of organized sequences such as sentences; all have rules for generating acceptable sentences; all have expandable lexicons. These assertions combine to form a point of view that de-emphasizes cognitive differences among different linguistic (cultural) groups.

Moreover, Noam Chomsky (1968) has developed a theory of grammar with profound implications for cross-cultural psychology. This theory maintains that all sentences—in their variety and uniqueness—are generated from a limited number of base components and a complex system of rules. Any human speaker who is competent in any human language, according to this theory, must store and use productive rules in a complex and nonmechanical fashion. The implication of this approach is that the cognitions or thinking processes of an individual cannot be less complex or constructive than the rules required for his speech production. Since there are no qualitative differences in the nature of language rules, it is impossible to conceive of more "simple" or more "advanced" cognitive levels.

Such analyses have been of great importance in countering those approaches that persist in characterizing the thought of nonliterate peoples in terms of its "deficiencies." Like the anthropological work on cognition, however, the linguists' objects of analysis are cultural in nature, and specifying the properties of language and communication systems does not in any way tell us about the actual operations of the individuals using the systems.

Psychological Approaches

Within psychology, the structural approach rests on a massive amount of experimental and observational data collected by Jean Piaget, the Swiss psychologist, on the thought processes of individual children. Piaget, who refers to himself as a genetic structuralist, is well known for his theory of intellectual growth. He sees the interaction between the individual child and the environment as giving rise to successive logical structures that regulate thinking processes (see Piaget and Inhelder, 1969). The characteristics of these structures and their order of appearance are considered to be universal. They are the outcome of adaptive processes between human organisms, whose biological heritage is the same the world over, and environments, whose fundamental physical properties (coordinates of space and time, behavior of objects under gravitational forces, and the like) are identical.

In earlier writings, the principal role Piaget assigned to culture was that of accelerating or retarding the developmental process—that is, introducing variations in the *ages* at which successive logical stages make their appearance. Such variations come about because cultures differ in the specific ways they handle the tasks of cultural and educational transmission and in the patterns of social interactions they provide. Thus, Piaget (1966) suggested that the developmental lag demonstrated between rural and urban children in Iran and elsewhere might be attributable either to the "general characteristics of social interactions" or to deficiencies in educational transmission.

More recently, Piaget has opened up the possibility that the "final" stage of development—that of formal, propositional thinking, which in Western cultures becomes elaborated during the age period of 12 to 15 years—might not appear at all, or might appear in more restricted and less general form, among cultures and individuals whose experience is limited to one or few technical or specialized occupational activities (1966, 1972). More extensive cross-cultural material is needed, he stresses, to follow up on the questions left unanswered by Levi-Strauss in respect to adult mentality:

> We would like to see cross-cultural studies of cognitive functions, which do not concern the child only, but development as a whole, including the final adult stages. When Levy-Bruhl raised the problem of the "pre-logic" of "primitive mentality," he undoubtedly overemphasized the opposition, in the same way as his posthumous recantation exaggerates perhaps in the other way the universality of structures. It seems to us that a series of questions remains unanswered by the excellent work of Levi-Strauss: for example, what is the operational level of adults in a tribal organization, as far as the technical intelligence (completely neglected by Levy-Bruhl), verbal intelligence, the solution of elementary logico-mathematical problems are concerned? The developmental data relative to the lower age levels will attain full significance only when we know the situation of the adults themselves. In particular, it is quite possible (and it is the impression given by the known ethnographic literature) that in numerous cultures, adult thinking does not proceed beyond the level of *concrete operations*, and does not reach that of propositional operations (1966, p. 13).

As this passage makes clear, Piaget's expanded view of the impact of culture on the "end point" of development still leaves intact a theoretical scheme that postulates a universal developmental process at lower age levels: at each level attained, the thought structures characteristic of that level are universal.

The popularity of Piaget's account of intellectual development in children has generated the single largest body of related research in the area of cross-cultural studies (see Dasen, 1972, and Goodnow, 1969, for reviews). In later chapters we shall discuss several of these studies and their bearing on the controversial issue of whether Piaget's theory does in fact identify universal thought structures or whether it simply builds a universal theory out of an examination of the logical structures of Western thought. What is of special interest in this theoretical review, however, is that approaches to culture and cognition such as Piaget's, which emphasize *universals*, have like those stressing *differences*, become increasingly more flexible and less absolute. Is there a possibility, then, of a synthesis that can incorporate cognitive sameness and differences in one coherent theory?

Soviet psychologists, working within a general framework of Marxist historical materialist theory, have been among those attempting to achieve such a synthesis. We will now turn briefly to a consideration of their views and the cross-cultural research they have generated.

Culture and Cognition: A Synthesis?

Since the early 1920s the Soviet psychologist L. S. Vygotsky and his students, among whom Alexander Luria is the most prominent, have developed an approach to the study of higher mental processes that stresses their *social-historical* character. This approach represents an attempt to extend to the domain of psychology Marx's thesis that man has no fixed human nature but continually makes himself and his consciousness through his productive activity:

> The way in which men produce their means of subsistence depends first of all on the nature of the actual means of subsistence they find in existence and have to reproduce. This mode of production must not be considered simply as being the production of the physical existence of these individuals. Rather it is a definite form of activity of these individuals, a definite form of expressing their life, a definite *mode of life* on their part. As individuals express their life, so they are (Marx and Engels, 1846, reprinted 1970, p. 42).

The central idea, so forcefully expressed in this passage, is that man's nature evolves as man works to transform Nature. The sweep of this concept—that both subject and object, man and his product, arise from a unitary process of activity—can best be grasped by an understanding of what Marx meant by *production*. Marx used the term to refer not only to the making of material products but to mental products as well (law, religion, metaphysics, and so on); similarly, *productive activity* encompasses not only manual but mental labor—labor in its broadest sense. Relating the production of ideas, conceptions, and consciousness to "material activity and the material intercourse of men" is the core of Marx's *materialism*. While Marx agreed that all men in all epochs engage in productive activity (that it is a general, universal process), he contended that in every time and place, the actual productive activity carried out is specific, concrete, and determined by the means of production at hand and the social relations among men to which they give rise. Thus, productive activity is a developing, historically determined process. Over the course of history ". . . men, developing their material production and their material intercourse alter, along with this their real existence, their thinking and the products of their thinking" (p. 47). This is the *historical* aspect of historical materialism.

A few quoted passages, of course, can do no more than suggest the depth and complexity of Marx's world outlook, an outlook that embraces but does not supercede the theories and methodologies of the various sciences. The very fact that this outlook emphasizes the complex, dynamic, and interrelated nature of all phenomena makes it impossible to simply extrapolate principles from Marx and apply them to the scientific question at issue. Thus, while psychologists and anthropologists working within a general Marxist perspective might agree on certain fundamental approaches, they often disagree vehemently in the way they elaborate them. It can be contended, for example, that the passage quoted above, referring to historical changes in thinking, applies only to the *contents* of men's conceptions and not to their thinking *processes*.

Vygotsky, however, maintained (and his views have given rise to the most sustained program of research) that changes occur in *process*. He tried to take account of both the general unchanging aspects of thinking processes and their specific, historically changing aspects by making a distinction between elementary psychophysical processes such as "sensation, movement, elementary forms of attentions and memory [which] are undoubtedly natural functions of the nervous tissue" and "higher psychological functions (voluntary memory, active attention, abstract thought and voluntary movement) [which] cannot be understood as a direct function of the brain" (Luria, 1971, p. 260). These higher processes are organized into *functional systems*, which arise in the course of historically determined practical and theoretical activities and change with the nature of these activities. The kinds of changes in activity that are presumed to make a difference in the structure of the higher mental processes are illustrated in the following description by Luria of conditions in certain isolated villages in Soviet Central Asia, where a psychological expedition was carried out in the 1930s:

> The non-technical economy (gardening, cotton-raising, animal hus-
> bandry) was replaced by more complex economic systems; there
> was a sharp increase in the communication with the cities; new
> people appeared in the villages; collective economy with joint plan-
> ning and with joint organization of production radically changed
> the previous economic activity; extensive educational and propa-
> ganda work intruded on the traditional views which previously had
> been determined by the simpler life of the village; a large network
> of schools designed to liquidate illiteracy was introduced to a
> large portion of the population and, in the course of a few years,
> the residents of these villages were included in a system of edu-
> cational institutions, and at the same time were introduced to a
> kind of theoretical activity which had previously not existed in
> those areas. . . .
> All of these events placed before psychology a fundamental ques-
> tion. Did these changes lead only to changes in the contents of
> conscious life or did they change the *forms* of consciousness as
> well? (1971, pp. 266, 267).

Experimental studies comparing traditional, nonliterate villagers with other residents of the same villages who had gone through a brief literacy course and who had participated in the newly formed collective farms found major differences in the way the two groups formed concepts and drew logical conclusions from verbal syllo-gisms:

> Not the abstract significance of words but concrete-practical ties
> reproduced from the experience of the subject play a direct role
> [among the nonliterate villagers]; not abstract thought, but visual-
> motor recollection determines the course of thinking. All of these
> facts have nothing in common with the biological features of the
> people that we have studied. They are a completely social-historical
> feature of psychological activity—it is only necessary for the
> social-historical conditions to change in order for these features
> of cognitive activity to change and disappear (1971, p. 269).

The implications of this social-historical view for developmental psychology have not been systematically explored. However, it suggests certain specific testable hypotheses about the relation be-tween cognition and particular social institutions and activities. In particular, Vygotsky's distinction between simple basic proc-esses and functional systems, which are composed of organized groupings of basic processes for application to particular cognitive problems, may offer the possibility of achieving a productive synthesis in cross-cultural theory and research.

Cognitive Capacities and Mental Tests

It might seem from the presentation thus far that arguments over primitive mentality and the evolution or development of mind have been a main concern of cross-cultural psychological investigations. This has certainly not been the case. Much of the psychological research, as we shall see, has been concerned with testing the generality of specific hypotheses about perception, language, and thought, and has frequently involved carrying overseas, in some adapted form, experimental questions and procedures that were created in the American laboratory or other institutional setting. Psychologists engaged in cross-cultural work have put heavy emphasis on formulating hypotheses that could be evaluated by *quantitative* means. Perhaps for this reason, comparative studies of mental capacities, using standardized tests, have long been popular and relatively numerous.

Research on mental capacities or abilities generally asks the question: Do these people (the group being studied) have less (or more) of a particular capacity than the group at home on which the test was standardized? It has too often been assumed that questions about the difference in some *capacity* ("intelligence" is the capacity most frequently investigated) are the same as questions about the difference in cognitive *process*. But this equation is not valid, as is vividly illustrated in the following passage from Levy-Bruhl, whom we presented as an advocate of irreconcilable differences between primitive and Western mentalities. Levy-Bruhl insisted that the differences in mentality that he described in no way justify the conclusion that primitive man is any less *intelligent* than his Western counterpart.

> Why is it that primitive mentality shows such indifference to, one might almost say such dislike of, the discursive operations of thought, of reasoning, and reflection, when to us they are the natural and almost continuous occupation of the human mind? *It is due neither to incapacity nor inaptitude* [italics added] since those who have drawn our attention to this feature of primitive mentality expressly state that among them are "minds quite as capable of scientific thought as those of Europeans," and we have

seen that Australian and Melanesian children learn what the missionary teaches them quite as readily as French or English children would do. Neither is it the result of profound intellectual torpor, of enervation and unconquerable weariness, for these same natives who find an insuperable difficulty in the very slightest abstract thought, and who never seem to reason, show themselves on the contrary observant, wise, skillful, clever, even subtle, when an object interests them (1923, pp. 29–30).

This is an important point to keep in mind, one that too often gets lost when observed differences are loosely interpreted in terms of hypothetical psychological entities like intelligence.

The first major comparative study of cognitive capacities was carried out jointly by anthropologists and psychologists among the inhabitants of the Torres Straits (between New Guinea and Australia) just before the turn of the century. W. H. R. Rivers and his colleagues conducted a wide variety of tests of perceptual function, as a result of which they concluded that perceptual *acuity* is not markedly different in the "savage" and the normal European. They explained the perceptual prowess attributed to nonliterate people by anthropologists as a result of the habit of attending to small details. This explanation is interesting for two reasons. First, it did *not* rest upon laboratory evidence. Second, it suggested that laboratory performance might not give a true picture of how well people could use their skills under other circumstances. This latter is an issue that will reverberate repeatedly in later research.

The work of Rivers and his colleagues also opened the question of possible cultural differences in the perception of color and in susceptibility to visual illusions, two problems that became the subject of a great deal of work in later years.

In the years just following World War I, interest in the testing of mental capacities shifted from the measurement of simple sensory functions to measurement of the higher functions; intelligence tests began to dominate the scene.

It is useful to remember that Binet and Simon began their work on the development of tests of mental ability in order to identify children not likely to profit from the kind of education offered in France at the start of this century. In the beginning, the tests were viewed quite pragmatically: Could they accurately predict whether or not a child would succeed in school? But very soon this practical question was mixed up with another, more theoretical question: Did the tests measure a fixed property of each child tested? Did the tests measure *intelligence?* Though Binet protested against those who regarded the test score as a fixed quantity, the principal American translators and users of his test from the outset claimed it was a measure of native ability, and early linked variations in score to "racially determined" mental capacities (Kamin, 1973). Much of the cross-cultural work on mental testing was inspired by the objective of discovering and measuring "racial" differences in intelligence, and to this day such tests are used to support claims of racial superiority of one people over another.

While the usefulness of carefully designed intelligence tests in predicting school performance has been repeatedly demonstrated, they have proved of little value as a technique for evaluating the relation between culture and mental processes. This is in part the result of conceptual difficulties: emphasis on race and the racial determinants of intelligence inevitably leads in the direction of de-emphasizing culture and social-environmental determinants of intelligence (see the discussion on race and culture in the early part of this chapter). Similarly, a concern with the measurement of *capacities* (how much verbal ability does A have compared with B) leads away from an examination of *process* (how does A go about solving this problem as compared with B?). In part the difficulties are methodological. Some of the basic problems in cross-cultural application of mental testing were summarized more than thirty years ago by Florence Goodenough, a leader in the field.

> Examination of the literature in this field over the past twenty years shows that approximately two-thirds of all the publications dealing with racial differences in mental traits have been concerned with the measurement of intelligence by means of tests designed for use with American or European whites. . . . Now the fact can hardly be too strongly emphasized that neither intelligence tests nor the so-called tests of personality and character are measuring devices, properly speaking. They are sampling devices.
>
> When, however, we leave the field of direct measurement, and endeavor to classify individuals or races on the basis of some presumably general trait that cannot be measured directly, we are faced with another and much more difficult problem of sampling. Not only must we be sure of the adequacy of our sampling of subjects, but we must also be sure that the test items from which the total trait is to be judged are *representative and valid samples of the ability in question, as it is displayed within the particular cul-*

ture with which we are concerned. The reason that the ordinary intelligence test works as well as it does for American urban populations is simply because the items of which it is composed are fairly representative samples of the kind of intellectual tasks that American city dwellers are likely to be called upon to perform. The principle involved is essentially the same as that employed by the thrifty housewife who takes a handful of beans out of the barrel from which she is to purchase a supply and judges the quality of the total on the basis of this sample. Considered as a sample, the intelligence test, with its variety of short tasks selected from out the infinite number that the individual is likely to be called upon to perform in the course of his daily life, differs from the handful of beans in only one important respect. The handful of beans is taken at random; the items comprising the intelligence test have been carefully selected with a view to their representativeness for the cultural requirements of the group for which the test was designed.

The wise housewife, engaged in a search for a good value in beans, would not make the mistake of judging the quality of one lot on the basis of a sample taken from another lot. She would not, moreover, make the further error of assuming that the standards applied to her judgment of beans are fully valid for the judgment of potatoes. Nevertheless, errors of both these types and particularly of the latter, are all too common in much of the published work on racial differences. A part of the difficulty, as I have indicated before, seems to be due to the unfortunate use of the term "measurement" in this connection. We may *measure* certain kinds of mental performance with an encouraging high degree of accuracy, regardless of the group upon which the measurement is taken. But the inferences to be drawn from such measurements will vary with circumstances (Goodenough, 1936, pp. 5, 6).

In addition to the important issues raised by Goodenough, psychologists critical of assuming that differences in test performance can be interpreted as differences in inherent capacities have pointed to a host of situational and nonintellective factors that are known to influence test performance. For example, LeVine (1970) lists such factors as fear of foreigners or adults who administer the tests, differential familiarity with the test situation or the task itself, or lack of interest. The reader can probably provide his own list of factors that, though they might produce differences in performance, he would not want to attribute to differences in intelligence.

These problems, combined with the fact that the test items have been picked for their success in predicting school performance rather than their diagnostic value as measures of particular kinds of psychological processes have led to a de-emphasis on the use of IQ tests as devices for studying cultural variations in cognitive processes. The limited usefulness of this line of work and the inherent difficulties in interpretation of IQ test data led us to exclude such research in the remainder of this book.

In the chapters that follow, we turn from grand theory to research. We will present the major lines of evidence currently available on the relation between culture and cognition, devoting each chapter to one particular cognitive area. In the final chapter, we will try to grapple with the problem of whether-and-how the research we have reviewed can illuminate the profound questions about human nature and human thought that lie at the base of all classical and contemporary explorations in this field.

chapter 3 *Culture and Language*

Any attempt to understand the relation between culture and cognition must consider the question of language at an early stage in the inquiry. Language is both the medium through which we obtain a great deal of our data concerning culture and cognition and, according to some theories, the major determinant of our thought processes.

The first point is obvious: almost all of our data concerning cultural differences in cognitive processes are obtained via verbal reports or other linguistic responses. Each of the examples given in the introduction makes use of linguistic evidence, although the particular nature of the evidence differs from case to case. This condition imposes on the investigator an obligation to disentangle those differences in performance that may be the result solely of linguistic differences from those caused by differences in the cognitive operations under investigation. We will deal with some of these difficulties and how they have been handled when we discuss the various problem areas that have been the subject of cross cultural research.

The second point requires extensive consideration. It is not only *not* obvious, it is counter to most of our intuitions. To say that language is a cause of the way we perceive or think seems to put the cart before the horse; most of us conceive of language as the vehicle through which we give expression to our perceptions and thoughts and look upon the particular language used for the purpose of expression as an unimportant accident of birth. Nevertheless, it can be argued that just the opposite relation holds true.

Linguistic Relativity: The Whorfian Hypothesis

Benjamin Whorf, an American authority on Indian languages, maintained that language is not a way of expressing or packaging thought but rather is a mold that shapes our thoughts. The world can be perceived and structured in many ways, and the language we learn as children directs the particular way we see and structure it. This view, which for many years was influential in the social sciences, is forcefully stated in the following passage by Whorf:

> It was found that the background linguistic system (in other words, the grammar) of each language is not merely a reproducing instrument for voicing ideas but rather is itself the shaper of ideas, the program and guide for the individual's mental activity, for his analysis of impressions, for his synthesis of his mental stock in trade. . . . We dissect nature along lines laid down by our native languages. The categories and types that we isolate from the world of phenomena we do not find there because they stare every observer in the face; on the contrary, the world is presented in a kaleidoscopic flux of impressions which has to be organized by our minds—and this means largely by the linguistic systems in our minds. We cut nature up, organize it into concepts, and ascribe significances as we do, largely because we are parties to an agreement to organize it in this way—an agreement that holds throughout our speech community and is codified in the patterns of our language. The agreement is, of course, an implicit and unstated one. *BUT ITS TERMS ARE ABSOLUTELY OBLIGATORY*; we cannot talk at all except by subscribing to the organization and classification of data which the agreement decrees. . . . We are thus introduced to a new principle of relativity, which holds that all

observers are not led by the same physical evidence to the same picture of the universe, unless their linguistic backgrounds are similar, or can in some way be calibrated (Whorf, 1956, pp. 212–214).

The Whorfian hypothesis of the language–cognition relationship actually contains two propositions, which are best analyzed separately. The first maintains that the world is differently experienced and conceived in different language communities. This proposition has come to be known as *linguistic relativity*. The second proposition goes beyond the simple statement that there are differences in cognition associated with differences in language to claim that language actually *causes* these differences. This doctrine of *linguistic determinism* is essentially a conception of a one-way causal sequence among cognitive processes with language playing the directing role.

This conception clearly transcends the issue of cultural differences in thought, which first intrigued Whorf, and zeroes in on a kernel problem in psychology. The question—Which is primary, language or conceptual thought?—has historically been, and to this day remains, one of the most controversial issues in psychology and one that has involved the world's leading developmental psychologists in theoretical combat. The language–thought problem provides a vivid illustration of how concern with cultural variation inevitably draws the social scientist into consideration of basic developmental processes that are presumed to occur in all human beings in all cultures.

Extreme forms of linguistic relativity and determinism would have serious implications, not only for mankind's study of himself, but for his study of nature as well, because it would close the door to objective knowledge once and for all. If the properties of the environment are known only through the infinitely varying selective and organizing mechanisms of language, what we perceive and experience is in some sense arbitrary. It is not necessarily related to what is "out there" but only to how our particular language community has agreed to *talk about* what is "out there." Our exploration of the universe would be restricted to the features coded by our language, and exchange of knowledge across cultures would be limited, if not impossible.

Perhaps it is fortunate that evidence related to the Whorfian hypothesis indicates that language is a less powerful factor in its constraints on perception and thought than Whorf believed it to be. It is most convenient to review the evidence in terms of the different aspects of language that Whorf thought might influence cognition. The first is the way in which individual units of meaning slice up the nonlinguistic world (the vocabulary or lexicon of a language). The second is "fashions of speaking," or rules for combining basic units of meaning (the grammar of a language). Whorf also suggested that these aspects of language were related both to other *cultural* characteristics (such as cultural attitudes toward time, toward quantification, and the like) and to *individual* characteristics (the single person's perception and thought).

The cultural phenomena that might be related to language characteristics are most commonly investigated by anthropologists, whereas individual behavior is primarily the province of psychologists. Because our aim in this book is to acquaint the reader with cross-cultural research in psychology, we will be reviewing only the data relating to the level of individual behavior. It is important that the reader keep in mind the fact that any generalizations suggested by this evidence do not necessarily apply to Whorf's insights about the integrated nature of various aspects of *culture,* nor do we mean to depreciate the importance of cultural analysis in its own right.

Our discussion will also be limited to the question of linguistic *relativity*—that is, that the world is differently experienced in different language communities—and will ignore the claim that language causes these differences. We think that propositions about causal relations among language, perception, and thought, such as those asserted by the doctrine of linguistic *determinism*, require study in a developmental perspective. To determine whether language or thought is the prior or more basic cognitive capacity, we would want to investigate how *changes* in either class of operations (linguistic or conceptual) affect the other. The cross-cultural data thus far collected on the Whorfian hypothesis are not of this kind. They are correlational in nature—that is, they show the association of one behavior with another, but they do not show whether either behavior causes or determines the other.

The Lexicon

Whorf's writings, supplemented by much anthropological data, contain numerous examples of how languages differ in the way their vocabularies segment the perceptual world. A classic illustration is the fact that languages vary widely in the number of color terms they possess and the parts of the color spectrum to which the terms refer. Some early observers of this phenomenon attributed the unfamiliar color categories to conceptual confusion on the part of their informants. When it was discovered that Homeric Greek, was deficient (by our standards) in color names, a debate ensued as to whether the early Greeks were color-blind. And, as we have seen, psychologists such as Werner have drawn conclusions about the "primitive" and "syncretic" level of perception among tribal peoples from an analysis of their color terms.

Here are some additional examples given by Whorf: The Hopi use a single word to name all flying things except birds (airplanes, insects, aviators), whereas our language has a separate word for each of these things. On the other hand, the Eskimo have many different words for snow—flying snow, slushy snow, dry snow—while we get along with one.

What is the significance of such lexical differences? Does the fact that a language does not have separate terms for certain phenomena mean that the users of this language are unable to distinguish these phenomena from others? Are Americans unable to see the differences that Eskimo see in snow? Or, to take an example that seems absurd on the face of it, is the Hopi unable to make a visual distinction between an aviator and an insect?

Certain aspects of language behavior challenge Whorf's thesis that the absence or presence of a lexical distinction can be taken as an indicator of a corresponding perceptual or conceptual distinction. His own linguistic behavior—his ability to translate the Eskimo terms for snow into English phrases—is evidence to the contrary. While it may not be possible to translate one language into another with term-for-term correspondence, while much may be lost in the process, the preservation and expression of at least some part of the original meaning argues against any hard-and-fast identification of word categories with thought categories. Nor is language interchangeability a skill confined to trained linguists; there are bilinguals among the general populace in most language communities. The importation of words from one language into another is a further example of the flexibility of languages in respect to vocabulary and a demonstration that the existing lexicon does not exhaust the discriminations of which the language users are capable. Rivers, in one of the earliest cross cultural studies in perception (Rivers, 1901) cites the example of Murray Islanders who had no indigenous term for the color blue but borrowed the English term and modified it to resemble the other members of their color vocabulary (*bulubulu*). On the basis of these facts and comparative language studies, the linguist Charles Hockett (1954, p. 122) has concluded that the question of lexical diversity can best be expressed as follows: Languages differ among themselves not so much as to what *can* be said in them but rather as to what it is relatively *easy to say*.

This formulation disposes of sweeping conclusions relating *all* lexical differences to differences in the way people perceive and think about the world, but it does not help us determine whether any *particular* set of distinctions encoded in a language lexicon are apprehended by individuals whose language lacks this set. To test this question requires some means of measuring perceptual and conceptual discriminations independently of language discriminations. If individuals give differential nonlinguistic responses to specifically different stimulus dimensions, we can infer that they are discriminating these dimensions even though they may lack terms in which to express them. An example would be accurate performance by a Zuni Indian in judging whether two colors in the orange-yellow range of the color spectrum are the same or different according to their measurable physical attributes in spite of the fact that his language does not contain separate terms for colors in this range. Since we know also that sometimes under a particular set of circumstances, individuals may not make distinctions they actually are capable of making, a further test would be a training experiment to determine whether individuals can learn to apply different lexical terms to classifications not expressed in their natural language. (See Heider, 1972, for the report of a successful learning experiment of this kind conducted among the Dani, a New Guinean population still living in a stone age culture.)

Most of the studies conducted by psychologists to test the impact of lexical distinctions on cognition have proceeded from the weaker version of the influence of vocabulary differences stated by Hockett (that it is *easier* to say something in one language than in another). Brown and Lenneberg (1954), who carried out one of the first experimental studies in this area, reasoned that the ease with which a distinction is expressed in a language is related to the frequency with which its referent perceptual discrimination is required in everyday life. For example, Eskimos are constantly required to make judgments about snows, whereas Americans may need to make such judgments only under rare and special circumstances. There should be a relation, then, between the more nameable perceptual categories and their availability for various cognitive operations, or as these authors put it, "The more nameable categories are nearer the top of the cognitive 'deck' " (p. 456).

For their perceptual domain they chose categories in the color space. Besides the classical interest in this domain, color space commended itself for investigation because it has been exhaustively mapped and measured and offers a set of physical dimensions against which varying color terminologies can be matched. The three dimensions of physical variation—hue, brightness, and saturation—are treated in the color space as continuous gradations that can be segmented more or less arbitrarily by language —a seemingly ideal representation of Whorf's general conception of the relation between language and reality.

Brown and Lenneberg chose memory as the cognitive process to relate to the linguistic variable of nameability or *codability*. Part of the way we remember an experience such as a color, they thought, is by remembering a word or name for it. Therefore, those color experiences that can be easily and adequately described in words should be more available in a memory test than others less easily verbalized.

Their first experiment was performed with English-speaking subjects on the assumption that a relation between codability and memory demonstrated within one language should also hold within other languages, and between languages as well. The subjects were presented with 24 color chips one at a time and instructed to name the color as quickly as possible. Several measures of the subjects' responses were found to be systematically related: the longer the name, the longer it took the subject to begin to say it and the less agreement there was among subjects in the terms used to name that particular color. The amount of naming agreement among subjects was selected as the most useful measure of codability.

The relation between codability and memory availability was then studied in a recognition experiment with a new group of subjects. Four of the 24 color chips were presented to a subject for a

5-second inspection period; then the chips were removed and the subject was asked to pick them out from an array of 120 colors. The number of correct identifications made by the subject was expressed as a recognition score. Under these circumstances there was a small correlation between codability (agreement on the name for a color) and recognition. When the memory task was made more difficult by introducing a delay period, filled with distracters, between the presentation of the color chips and their later identification, the correlation was much stronger. When the memory task was simplified by presenting one color for later identification and by having an immediate recognition test, the correlation almost vanished. Under these latter conditions a measure of *visual discriminability* correlated significantly with recognition, emphasizing the close relation between the physical event and memory instead of the relation between language and memory.

The relation between codability and recognition under difficult memory conditions was confirmed in a second study (Lenneberg and Roberts, 1956) conducted among the Zuni Indians of the southwestern United States. The authors hypothesized that the Zuni would have trouble remembering colors in the yellow-orange section of the color spectrum, since their language does not distinguish between these two colors. In this carefully conducted experiment, they found that monolingual Zuni did indeed make the most errors in recognition of these colors followed by subjects who spoke both Zuni and English, with monolingual English-speakers making the fewest errors.

These experiments were widely quoted as evidence for a weak version of linguistic relativity. But further investigation showed that the demonstrated relation between codability and recognition did not hold up for all colors. Burnham and Clark (1955) secured recognition data for another array of colors that did not differ as distinctively in hue as the array in the original study. Lenneberg (1961) took these recognition data and correlated them with codability data he had secured independently for this color array. He found that correlation was a negative one—the better the naming agreement, the lower the recognition score! Evidently, a short distinctive lexical term like *blue* is useful for remembering a color blue when it is surrounded by colors of distinctive hues (red, yellow, green, etc.), but it does not help in the selection of a particular blue from an array of blues of different brightnesses and saturations. Here a phrase—"the cloudy blue with a gray tinge" —may be more useful.

In an attempt to resolve this contradiction, Lantz and Stefflre (1964) developed a new method of measuring codability which they called *communication accuracy*. Viewing memory as a situation in which an individual communicates to himself through time, they argued that items communicated accurately *inter*personally (that is, to another person) would also be more accurately communicated *intra*personally (to oneself). They presented test colors to a group of subjects who were asked to describe them in such a way as to enable others to pick them out of an array. The descriptions were then read to a second group who tried to find the colors from among the recognition array. This procedure yielded very high and statistically significant correlations between communication accuracy and recognition scores for *both* the Brown-Lenneberg and Burnham-Clark color arrays. On the other hand, communication accuracy and naming agreement (the original measure of codability) were not highly correlated.

These results were replicated and extended for non-English-speakers in a study by Stefflre, Vales, and Morely (1966) conducted in Yucatan, Mexico. They worked with two different language groups—Mayan Indians, whose native language, Yucatec, contains relatively few color terms, and students at the University of Yucatan, whose native language, Spanish, has a color vocabulary similar to English.

For each language group a clear correlation was established between communication accuracy for particular colors and the errors that subjects *within that language* made when trying to recognize colors a short time later. The speakers of the two languages found different colors easy to communicate, so that the recognition errors of Yucatec-speakers were not the same as those of Spanish-speakers. Here is clear evidence that errors in recognition are associated with the linguistic, or communication, code more strongly than with the physical attributes of the colors being recognized.

The same general results were obtained by Wang (1972) using the Lantz and Stefflre technique with American college students. Wang first obtained communication accuracy scores for a large set of colors. Then for each color he picked two color names that produced low accuracy; one of the two names biased selection to one side of the test color, the other to the opposite side. When a new group of subjects was presented the colors using the biasing color names, recognition scores were found to err in the direction predictable from the name.

Lantz and Stefflre explained the superiority of the communication measure in predicting recognition scores by the fact that it allows flexibility in the particular verbal expression (single- or multi-word name, phrase, etc.) used to characterize the target stimulus.

> The kind of formulation presented here of relation between language and behavior emphasizes the productivity of language—*new descriptions may be formed spontaneously* [italics added] and function to encode stimuli effectively. . . . Any description of the relation between language and behavior or language and thought that does not take this into account and emphasizes only the role of dictionary words and/or the grammatical categories will find it difficult to deal with the facts found in a particular experimental context (Lantz and Stefflre, 1964, p. 481).

In addition to their contribution to the language–cognition problem, the Lantz-Stefflre study shows the limitations of any attempt to relate cognitive behavior to *static* characteristics of language without taking into account the dynamic functions that language can serve within various problem-solving situations. Their communication measure points to a whole new set of language variables connected with language *use* that might be expected to influence cognition. If *intra*personal communication is related to *inter*personal communication, then the social processes of communication within various cultures need to be studied: What form do they take and what aspects of experience are most commonly verbalized and communicated? Looking back at the original Brown-Lenneberg study, we note that their hypothesis of the relationship between codability and memory rested on the assumption their subjects actively applied and stored verbal labels for the test colors. This, too, is an instance of language *use* in a particular situation and an additional demonstration of the fact that the activities of the subject are a crucial intervening variable in attempts to test language–cognition relationships.

In the last few years, the linguistic relativity thesis has been challenged even within the color domain. As we have indicated, the color space was long considered a source of uniform, physical variation, which languages partition arbitrarily into color-name categories. Research conducted by two anthropologists (Berlin and Kay, 1969) suggests that this is not the case. They asked speakers of 20 different languages to choose the best examples of their languages' basic color terms from an array of color chips, and to indicate, in addition, all the chips that could be called by that name. As expected, the boundaries of the color terms varied widely, but the best examples (Berlin and Kay called them the *focal colors*) were stable; instead of being randomly distributed throughout the array they were tightly clustered around 11 basic colors—8 chromatic colors, whose English names are *red, yellow, green, blue, brown, orange, pink,* and *purple*—and 3 achromatic colors, *black, white,* and *gray.* Berlin and Kay argue that the emphasis on cross-cultural differences in linguistic encoding of colors has stemmed from investigators' preoccupation with variable color *boundaries* to the neglect of common *focal color referents.*

In a series of studies, Heider (1972), explored the psychological implications of these reputedly universal focal colors. After refining the location of each of the focal colors in the color space, she tested to see whether these colors were the most codable *across language families.* Subjects spoke languages belonging to the Indo-European, Austronesian, Sino-Tibetan, and Afro-Asiatic families, plus Hungarian, and Japanese. The results were quite clear: focal colors were given shorter names and were named more quickly than nonfocal colors (the two measures of codability used in this study). A third study, modeled after the Brown-Lenneberg experiments demonstrated that focal colors could be remembered more accurately than nonfocal colors *even by speakers of a language that lacks basic hue terms.* The Dani of New Guinea, whose color lexicon is restricted to two basic terms meaning, roughly, dark and light, showed memory superiority for focal colors over nonfocal colors similar to that shown by the comparison group of American subjects whose language has a term for each member of the entire set of focal colors. What does this imply about the role of language in this task? Data from another series of experiments (Heider and Olivier, 1972) has led Heider to conclude that there may be a *visual* rehearsal process in the recognition task which is separable from a *verbal* rehearsal process. Visual memory images may be isomorphic to visual images of colors that are physically present, and thus more responsive to perceptually salient characteristics of the stimuli and more resistant to language-related distortion. In Brown and Lenneberg's easy memory task, recognition could be accounted for, as we have seen, by the perceptual property of discriminability. Just which memory tasks call out visual rather than verbal memory processes in which populations, what the nature of the interaction may be between these two processes and what kind of "verbal encoding" is employed in a given situation are all important questions which studies of this kind must answer.

It is interesting to observe how a line of research originally inspired by notions of linguistic relativity has now led to the claim that there are certain universals or invariants in the relation between one area of perceptual experience and language lexicons. In spite of the great variety of terms for colors and the unstable boundaries separating one color class from another, certain colors seem to be universally salient and easier to remember. On the strength of this evidence Heider (1972) suggests that the customary understanding of the relationship between language terms and concepts may be the reverse of what it is customarily understood to be. "In short, far from being a domain well suited to the study of the effects of language on thought, the color space would seem to be a prime example of the influence of underlying perceptual-cognitive factors on the formation and reference of linguistic categories" (p. 20).

Grammar

Not only do languages differ with respect to the way in which their vocabularies cut up the world, they also differ with respect to the way in which individual units of meaning get combined. Whorf was especially fascinated by these structural features of language, which he called "fashions of speaking," and he emphasized their importance in molding, unconsciously, the language community's view of reality. He pointed out, for example, that English verbs take different forms in accordance with the temporal distinctions, past, present, and future. These obligatory temporal references fit in with our culture's concept of time as a never-ending line and our preoccupation with its measurement (as witness our calendars and clocks in almost infinite variety). However, Hopi words that function as verbs—including words that we clearly treat as nouns, such as lightning and puff-of-smoke

—emphasize duration rather than time of occurrence. Another example of a structural fashion of speaking is supplied by Lee (1938), who describes verbs in the Wintu (California Indian) language as being classified by "validity modes." If the event being spoken of is a matter of hearsay, one word is used; if it is an event actually observed by the *speaker* (not the subject of the sentence), another verb is used. Hence, different words for *to hear* might be used by a witness to a crime who "heard" the gun go off and by the policeman relating the witness's claim of having "heard" the gun go off.

As in the case of the linguistic evidence relating to lexical differences, we are not sure what to make of these instances. Whorf and others would have us believe that they reflect inescapable constraints on our thinking, but the evidence relevant to thought is all via language; no independent indicator of cognition is offered. We have to infer thought processes from general cultural indices (whose meaning we find it difficult to agree upon) or from other linguistic evidence, which we also believe to be related to cognition. In either event we are treading on very thin ice.

We know of only two experiments that present nonlinguistic evidence relevant to the influence of grammar on cognitive activities. The first was conducted by Carroll and Casagrande (1958) on a Navaho Indian reservation. In the Navaho language certain verbs that refer to manipulation of things require special forms, depending on what kind of thing is being handled: there is one verb form if the object is round and thin, another for a long flexible object, still another for a long rigid object, and so on. Since the Navaho grammar forces attention to the shape, form, and material of things, it is reasonable to assume that the behavior of Navahos toward things might be guided by these particular attributes to a greater extent than is the behavior of non-Navaho speakers. So Carroll and Casagrande reasoned.

They chose to investigate the saliency of these attributes in the object-sorting behavior of matched age groups of Navaho children, one speaking only Navaho, the other speaking only English. The children's actual task was to match an object with one of a pair of objects shown by the experimenter. A presentation pair might be a yellow rope and a blue stick, as shown in Figure 3–1. The child would then be shown a yellow stick and asked which one of the presentation pair it belonged with. Results con-

Show the child:

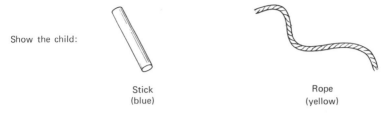

Stick	Rope
(blue)	(yellow)

Figure 3-1. Objects used to study the influence of grammar on cognition (fashioned after Carroll and Casagrande, 1958).

firmed expectations about attribute saliency: Navaho-speaking children tended to match the items on the basis of form rather than color at younger ages than the English-speaking children did. Unhappily for the theory, when the same matching task was given to middle-class English-speaking children in metropolitan Boston, they too showed a preference for form over color—a preference that Carroll and Casagrande accounted for by the abundant experience with shapes and forms which these children had acquired in the course of playing with toys. They concluded that in this particular task, form choices could be mediated by *either* language or nonlanguage experience and that, overall, the results show that grammatical categories do influence matching. Note, however, that this is a very benign form of linguistic relativity, much more consistent with the idea that concepts are differentially available in different cultures rather than with the idea that they are exclusive to some one particular culture.

A recent experiment by Cole and his associates (1969) reinforces this interpretation. Their experiment took advantage of the fact that in the Kpelle language of Liberia, comparisons of size are not symmetric as they are in English. Thus, in comparing a large and a small person, a Kpelle would always refer to the larger, his remark translating as "John, he is big past Joe." Although it is possible for him to say the equivalent of "Joe is smaller than John," the Kpelle expression translates as "Joe, in smallness surpasses John," and it is rarely if ever used.

This observation was combined with a standard experiment, known as a *transposition experiment*, which has been used extensively to study the development of conceptual behavior in children. The experiment is most easily understood when we consider a particular example, such as that shown in Figure 3–2.

1. Train the child that the large block is correct.

2. Then test on one of the following pairs.

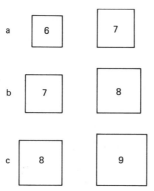

Figure 3-2. Design for a transposition experiment.

In this example, the child is first taught always to choose the larger of two blocks presented to him by the experimenter. In successive trials the physical placement of the two blocks is randomized so that size is the only reliable cue for determining which block is correct. After the subject reliably picks the correct block, he is presented with two other blocks also different in size. The question is: Will the subject choose the block that is the same size (or closest to the same size) as the block that was correct during training, or will he pick the block that bears the same size *relation* to its paired mate as the correct block did to its mate during training? For example, if, as shown in Figure 3–2, block 6, the larger block, is correct during training, then when the subject is presented with the pair of blocks 6 and 7 (condition A) will he choose 6 (the same) or 7 (the larger)? When the block bearing the correct size relation is chosen, the subject is said to show transposition.

Three groups of Kpelle children participated in the experiment:

monolingual Kpelle-speaking children aged 4 to 6, nonliterate children aged 6 to 8 who spoke a little English in addition to Kpelle, and 6 to 8-year-old first-graders who could speak a good deal of English and who were beginning to read and write. The same blocks and the same testing procedures were used also with a group of 4- to 5-year-old American nursery school children.

When the experiment was actually run, some groups were trained to choose the smaller block and others to choose the larger, and they were tested on different combinations of smaller or larger blocks. If the Kpelle are used to making size comparisons by singling out the larger member first, we might expect monolingual Kpelle speakers to learn the larger-than relationship faster and to transpose it to test trials more readily than any of the other comparison groups. But this was not the case. Virtually all of the children showed transposition, regardless of their language and school background, and regardless of whether they were being tested on the larger-than or the smaller-than relationship. Moreover, learning to choose the larger block during training was no more rapid than learning to choose the smaller block.

These findings imply that the Kpelle preference for comparing the larger of two things to the smaller has no influence on discrimination learning. Here, as in the work reported earlier on perception of focal colors, we seem to be dealing with stimulus properties and relationships that exert a strong control over behavior. Two aspects of the Kpelle children's behavior in this task did seem affected, however. On the very first trial of training, before the subject had any information about the problem, all the Kpelle children showed a significant preference for the larger block, while the American children did not. Second, when the test phase was over and subjects were asked why they had made the choices they did, Kpelle subjects were better able to justify their responses if they were trained to choose the larger block, but American subjects showed no difference in the adequacy of their justifications as a function of which training block was correct.

Like the result of Carroll and Casagrande's research, and in fact like virtually all of the experimentally derived results relating to language and cognition in a cross-cultural context, these data point to limitations on the generality of the linguistic relativity hypothesis. We will defer any attempt to summarize the present status of the hypothesis until we look briefly at some proposals that all languages, in spite of their heterogeneity, share certain *common* ways of coding experience. These propositions constitute a hypothesis about *linguistic universality.*

Linguistic Universality

The Whorfian hypothesis is primarily concerned with the referential aspect of language: how it maps experience, what it points to (denotative meaning). But there is another aspect of language, which expresses the qualities of experience—the feelings, images, and relationships that words arouse (sometimes referred to as connotative meaning). One of the largest, most systematic, and sustained cross-cultural investigations of language and thought in the last decade has been concerned with testing the generality of this aspect of meaning. With the help of cooperating social scientists in twelve countries (Japan, Hong Kong, India, Afghanistan, Iran, Lebanon, Yugoslavia, Poland, Finland, Holland, Belgium, and France), Charles Osgood (1964), a leading American psycholinguist, has been studying affective meaning systems through the use of a special measuring instrument he devised, called the *semantic differential.*

The basic procedure of the semantic differential is this: a subject is presented with a list of verbal concepts: *mother, bread, communism, teacher,* for example. Then he is given a list of antonym qualifiers (represented by adjectives in English) such as *good–bad, honest–dishonest, hot–cold.* The subject has to rate each concept against each qualifier pair using a number from 1 to 7, with the 1 standing for an extreme quality of the left-hand member of the pair (*good* in the first example given), the 7 for an extreme quality of the right-hand member of the pair (*bad*), and the other numbers for intermediate qualities. In a dozen or more factorial studies conducted with American English-speaking subjects, Osgood and his associates kept finding that the rating results could be described in terms of three dominant factors or dimensions of meaning: an *evaluative* factor (represented by scales like *good–bad*); a *potency* factor (represented by scales like *strong–weak*); and an *activity* factor (represented by scales like *fast–slow*). The problem then arose: Is this semantic framework limited to Americans speaking the English language or is it "shared by all humans regardless of their language or culture?" To find out, Osgood and his associates prepared a list of 100 familiar concepts that had been selected by linguists and anthropologists as "culture fair." This list was translated into the indigenous language, and from then on the work was conducted entirely in the various native tongues. Qualifiers and their opposites were elicited from groups of high school boys in each country. Scales were constructed, based on their responses, and then new groups of subjects were asked to rate the original 100 concepts against these scales.

The results to date indicate that the same three dimensions of meaning (evaluation, potency, and activity) describe the rating judgments in all the languages studied, although individual concepts are rated differently from culture to culture on these semantic factors. Stated a little differently, the structure of connotative meaning is the same from culture to culture, while the connotative meanings of particular concepts are culture specific. Osgood attributes this aspect of linguistic universality to the fact that his scales tap emotional feelings mediated by the affective nervous system which is "panhuman biologically" (Osgood, 1963, p. 320). A limitation in respect to "universality" to which we might draw attention is that his subject populations were all *educated* groups. In view of the strong homogenizing influence of education on the performance of cognitive tasks, to be described in later chapters, this restriction may be quite important.

Osgood goes on to suggest that universality of affective meaning systems may also account for the phenomena of metaphor
and *verbal–visual synesthesia.* A classic study on metaphor conducted by Asch (1961) investigated how terms referring to physical properties of things *(hard, straight, hot)* are used to characterize psychological attributes of persons ("John is a very cold person"). He found strikingly similar metaphoric applications in such dissimilar languages as Hebrew, Greek, Chinese, Thai, Hausa, and Burmese.

Verbal–visual synethesia is a phenomenon in which words are regularly paired with certain pictorial representations rather than with others, as in the pairing of *happy* with an arrow pointing upward instead of downward. This was one of the fascinating results found by Osgood in a cross-cultural study demonstrating the generality of visual–verbal synesthetic tendencies among Navaho, Mexican-Spanish, Anglo, and Japanese subjects (1960).

Somewhat more research has been devoted to another related

phenomenon known as *phonetic symbolism*—the appropriateness of the relation between the sound of a word and its meaning. The *tinkle* of an icecube in a glass or the *boom* of the drum in the Salvation Army band might be considered to have appropriate verbal expression in the sense that the word sounds help to communicate some attributes of their referents.

Edward Sapir initiated research in phonetic symbolism in the 1920s by using a vocabulary of artificial words. (His and other early work are reviewed in Brown, 1958, Chap. 4). Brown, Black, and Horowitz (1955) carried out a well-controlled, specifically cross-language study which begat a series of investigations still under way. Twenty-one pairs of English antonyms *(warm–cold, heavy–light)* were translated into Chinese, Czech, and Hindi and were given to American college students unfamiliar with these languages. Told only the dimensions along which the words varied, the students were able to make better-than-chance discriminations concerning the meanings of the individual words in all three languages. To illustrate: given the pair of Chinese words *ch'ing* and *ch'ung* and the information that one means light and the other heavy, subjects tended to correctly guess *ch'ing* as light.

In many variations of this task using different languages and different methods of word presentation, investigators have repeatedly demonstrated above-chance matching of word meaning to word form. Correct matchings have been made even when each of the two members of a word pair was presented in a different language—*light* in Czech and *heavy* in Japanese, for example (Klank, Huang, and Johnson, 1971). A start has been made in identifying *which* sounds give cues to *which* meanings. Some evidence links vowel sound to meanings of magnitude: it has been found that high and front vowels occur proportionately more often in words denoting smallness, and low back vowels in words denoting largeness in *both* Chinese and English.

The first indication that the correspondence between the sound of a word and its meaning may influence cognitive processes comes from a recently reported Russian study on verbal memory (Baihdurashvili, 1972). Two groups of subjects were required to memorize lists of word pairs composed of a Japanese word and a word in the subject's native language. For the first group, the Japanese word was paired with a native word of the same meaning; the second group had a list in which the same Japanese words were paired with native words of different meanings. The first group learned more rapidly and showed greater retention of the material, evidencing, in the investigator's words, "the lawful character of naming in a natural language" (p. 411).

Taken together, work in the semantic differential, synesthesia, metaphor, and phonetic symbolism seem to offer impressive support for the argument that certain qualities of experience are given common expression in many languages and cultures, differ as they may among themselves in other characteristics.

At this point we might stop to consider for a moment the implications of work in *language universals*, which we mentioned briefly in Chapter 2.

Joseph Greenberg (1966), G. A. Miller (1970), and others have singled out for attention various features of phonology (sound systems), grammar, and lexicon that all languages seem to share. Miller refers to these as "general design features" of language and suggests that their existence points to common physiological and psychological processes or capacities shared by all men. Chomsky (1968) maintains that these commonly shared features are themselves derived from base structures, which are built-in components of the human mind. These base structures make possible, and at the same time constrain, all language development. The task of psychology, he contends, is to search out the nature of these mental mechanisms underlying linguistic competence. But while it may be relatively simple to identify the basic mechanisms accounting for universal features in phonology (the limited variety of articulates possible to human speech apparatus, for example), it is another matter entirely to identify the psychological processes that might account for universals in grammar and lexicon. To add to the difficulty, the question of the relation between underlying psychological processes and linguistic competence has become the subject of a nonproductive debate pitting genetic innate mechanisms against learning mechanisms. On the other hand, developmental psycholinguists, studying the acquisition of language in the first few years of the child's life, are contributing information suggesting that there may be certain sequences in language mastery that are independent of features of particular languages (Smith and Miller, 1966) and that might at some future time help to elucidate the question of language universals. Fundamentally important as these issues are, we will not explore them further in this discussion because they revolve around a somewhat different question from that concerning us. Chomsky, Miller, and others are asking the question: What are the cognitive operations underlying the acquisition and use of language? In other words, what capacities do we need in order to speak? The problem tackled in this chapter has been that of specifying the interrelations *between* language processes and other cognitive operations: How are speech and thinking related to each other?

Summary

Our review of the research evidence bearing on the Whorfian hypothesis certainly makes untenable any strong version of linguistic relativity. It is probable that the majority of scholars would agree in rejecting those of Whorf's formulations that stress the *arbitrary* character of the language–experience relationship and the inescapable and rigid constraints imposed on cognitive processes by language. Yet in spite of the patchiness of the evidence, few would be likely to allow linguistic relativity no role whatsoever. Here are some of the reasons we would give for keeping the question open.

1. First we would want to stress the limited nature of the experimental operations that have been brought to bear on the hypothesis. While there were good reasons for choosing to investigate linguistic relativity through color terminology, the superior intelligence of hindsight suggests this may have been something short of an ideal strategy. It is very likely that the expression of perceptual experience is most constrained by certain salient and stable stimulus attributes and is less responsive to the variability introduced by language. It may very well be that the "filtering effect" of language is greatest in respect to domains of phenomena that are definable, not in terms of physical properties, but in terms of attributes that are culturally specified. One thinks of such domains as social roles, for example; attributes defining categories of people (unlike those defining colors) are assigned by culture not nature. Or consider the area of ideology or theoretical work in general, where concepts largely acquire their meanings through their being embedded in explanatory verbal networks. It is here that language may play the greatest role in shaping the person's view of reality, in influencing his memory and thinking processes, and in contributing to his understanding or misunderstanding of other cultures. But such a proposition brings us around full circle to the difficulty with which we started: Can this hypothesis be tested empirically, and how?

2. A second point that should be made is that the demonstration of universal relations between aspects of language and cognition does not automatically make moot the question of culturally relative differences. Nor is it necessarily paradoxical that there should be both universals and differences in any domain of human experience. By now it is clear that the relations between language and cognition are not likely to be exhausted in a few general propositions. The growing body of research dealing with language and thought is uncovering multiple and complex interrelations between them. Our understanding will grow as theoretical work and cross-cultural research succeed in elaborating these multiple relations in both their universal *and* their particular aspects.

3. Finally, while Whorf's view of the particular characteristics of language important for cognition has not been disproved, there appear to be more fruitful ways today of investigating the classic questions. In our analysis of the Brown-Lenneberg experiments on color codability and memory (pp. 45–46) we pointed out that the hypothesized effects of language operated only through some assumed *verbal activity* on the part of the subject. None of the experimenters suggested that the vocabulary item as a static piece of information was responsible for the accuracy of recognition; all stressed what the subject did with it. These observations led us to point out the possible important implications of different *uses* of language for cognition. This indeed has been a subject of intensive research in the last few years, although not in the area traditionally designated as cross-cultural; this research has been stimulated by social class and subcultural comparisons within one society (principally the United States and England). A new field of *sociolinguistics* is showing rapid growth, its credo being that language cannot be understood except in its use functions—as human communication sensitive to the social contexts in which it is carried out. One of the seminal thinkers in this field, Basil Bernstein, has delineated different forms of speech codes that he considers characteristic of the English working class and English middle class, respectively, and that he feels significantly affect their learning experiences (1972). Bernstein has been concerned with how members of certain social strata develop characteristic ways of using speech to communicate with one another. This is seemingly a far cry from the characteristics of language that interested Whorf, but Bernstein specifically acknowledges his debt to Whorf for alerting him to the "selective effect of culture (acting through its patterning of social relationships) upon the *patterning* of grammar together with the pattern's semantic and thus cognitive significance" (1972, p. 224). In this young and potentially rich field of investigation of how individuals use their language not only for social communication but as a tool for thought, Whorf still lives.

chapter 4 *Culture and Perception*

"Primitives perceive nothing in the same way as we do," said Levy-Bruhl (1910, p. 30) and while it is clear that his controversial conclusion was based on inadequate evidence, more recent efforts to get adequate evidence about what people in other cultures "see" have continued to be dogged with difficulties and disputation.

A problem we face at the outset is the varied usage of the term *perception* in the psychological and anthropological literature. Chapter 3 should serve to make us cautious about how we interpret certain words, such as *blue*, which may have different referents in two languages. But the problems relating to the term *perception* are much deeper than the question of language referents.

When psychologists use the word *perception*, they generally refer to processes by which people organize and experience information that is primarily of sensory origin. They also commonly emphasize that perception involves active operations on information and is not a passively received "direct copy" of the external world. Anthropologists and laymen, however, tend to use the word *perception* in a much broader sense, to refer not only to the organization of sensory data but to such phenomena as outlook on life, world view, interpretation of events, and the like. In the work to be reviewed in this chapter, we will be speaking of perception in the narrower, psychological sense. We will deal with some of the issues involved in the broader definition in later chapters where we discuss classification and conception.

But perception in the narrow sense has also been a source of theoretical conflict within psychology from its inception. One of the earliest major controversies pitting the titans of psychology against one another concerned the nature of perceptual experience (Boring, 1950): well-trained observers from different laboratories reported different perceptual experiences under identical stimulus conditions. The disillusionment that followed years of unresolved arguments was a major impetus to a shift in research strategy among psychologists. Instead of attempting to make inferences about perceptual experience on the basis of introspective reports, they tried to get at experience through the use of behavioral indicators. As we shall see, this methodological reform did not dispose of the problems of inference and interpretation of data from perception experiments.

However, even in the heyday of early psychological research on perception, cross-cultural research seemed an attractive possibility to some investigators. While recognizing the new difficulties introduced by language and custom, studies of different cultural groups, especially non-European peoples, seemed to offer a means of resolving several perennial debates among psychologists and philosophers. Primary among these was the nativist–empiricist issue: Are the basic perceptual catgories (constancies, figure-ground perception, and the like) innate or the result of experience? Of equal interest in the post-Darwinian era was the possibility of discovering something about the evolution of mental capacities. This was one of the motivations leading to Rivers's perceptual investigations in the Torres Straits in 1901, mentioned in Chapter 2.

In the tradition of Spencer and others, Rivers and his colleagues speculated that certain senses might be more highly developed among primitive people than among industrialized people. They put these speculations to the test by carrying the instruments and techniques developed in the new experimental psychology laboratories to anthropological field stations on the Papua Coast and in southern India. Here they collected a large number of systematic observations on vision, hearing, and other sense modalities, using diversified tasks and measurement procedures. Reviewing the data on visual acuity, Rivers concluded that there was little basis for prior beliefs that sensory acuity was better among non-Western people. He did not, however, draw the additional conclusion that the observations on which these beliefs were based were erroneous. Rather, he argued that it *appeared* as though primitive people had exceptional sensory powers because they devoted their attention predominantly to "objects of sense," making minute discriminations among the details of landscape, vegetation, and animal life, which are made in our society only by zoologists and botanists. He also clung to Spencer's hypothesis that highly refined and discriminatory powers of observation were attained at the cost of the higher mental faculties. "If too much energy is expended on the sensory foundations, it is natural that the intellectual superstructure should suffer" (Rivers, 1901, pp. 44, 45).

Rivers's data, though not his extrapolations from it, were largely accepted by psychologists, and little systematic work has been done since that time on comparative sensory capacities. Attention has shifted to more sophisticated questions about the influence of cultural and environmental experiences on perception. In reviewing this work, though, we are struck by the fact that only a small set of the problems investigated in European and American laboratories during the past hundred years has been submitted to cross-cultural analysis. The specific questions that have been popular research topics during the past two decades of heavy activity have emphasized cultural differences in very restricted domains of perceptual experience. Before we look at these questions in detail, we need to point out that all cross-cultural research on cultural differences in perception rests on the assumption that commonalities in perceptual processes among peoples of the world far outweigh whatever differences may be found. This simple fact tends to be forgotten in the search for variation. But its truth is evident—it would be impossible to test for *differences* if there were not a commonly shared perceptual foundation to use as a starting point. It is taken for granted, for example, that everyone possesses form and depth perception in the real visual world, no matter how they perform on perceptual tests making use of special stimuli (whether they show 3-D perception in viewing photographs, for example).

The research questions most actively pursued today include the following:

1. Are there experiences that influence the perception of artificial visual representations (like photographs and drawings)?

2. Do different experiences lead to alternative ways of organizing ambiguous or deceptive stimuli?

3. Does growing up in a particular cultural environment predispose a person to select specific features of his environment for special attention so that they are seen more clearly or quickly than others?

In looking at psychologists' answers to these and related problems, we will concentrate on a few techniques that have received the most attention and that therefore present the most solid cases for study.

Pictorial Depth Perception

From time to time one reads the reports of travelers indicating that native informants fail to recognize the contents of photographs, even when the pictures are taken in the informant's locale and even if the pictures are of the informant or members of his family.

Such is the case in central Liberia, where nonliterate, traditional Kpelle rice farmers were shown the pictures in Figure 4–1. Looking at the photographs we can think of various reasons why naive subjects who had not previously seen such pictorial representations of real objects might be confused. The perspective of the mat upon which the objects rest is represented by the up-down dimension of the picture, a convention that we take for granted, but which is by no means inborn. We need only recall that it was not until the fifteenth century that such conventions became a part of Western artistic work; the use of perspective to represent distance became a full-blown feature of the Western tradition with Leonardo da Vinci. (For pre-da Vinci distance

Figure 4-1. Photographs shown to Kpelle rice farmers in Liberia, Africa.

representation, see Figure 4–2.) Even today the use of perspective is by no means worldwide, and some modern Western painters deliberately violate the conventions to obtain particular artistic effects. The various cues in paintings and photographs, which we take for granted, took centuries to develop; it requires some measure of experience on the part of an individual before three-dimensional perceptions of pictures becomes natural.

The items shown in Figure 4–1 are also presented apart from

Figure 4-2.   Fifteenth century Italian artist Di Paolo shows people in the distance larger than those in foreground.

their habitual contexts, and the colors are not perfectly true to life. Considerable systematic research is needed to disentangle the many possibilities that could account for the difficulties of interpretation experienced by naive observers of photographs or other two-dimensional pictures.

On certain questions of interpretation, research has been considerable but not systematic. On the most elementary level, one would want to know what factors are involved in grasping the notion that lines, colors, or black, gray and white shadings on paper represent anything at all. Such a notion must underlie the identification of what is represented. An oft-quoted observation by Herskovits describes a bush woman's confusion when presented with a photograph of her son, how she turned the piece of paper this way and that, not knowing what to do with it. When Herskovits pointed out the details of the photograph, however, she perceived the subject (cited in Segall, Campbell, and Herskovits, 1966). There is impressive evidence that those who have the notion that known things may be represented on paper can identify the things under conditions of representation that do not involve the use of conventionalized cues (we will discuss these later). For example, Brimble (1963) presented Bantu villagers with 40 simple line drawings of familiar things and secured correct identifications in over 90 percent of the cases. Deregowski (1968a) found that Zambian adults and children, when shown extremely simplified photographs of animal models against a neutral background, could select the correct match from an array of the actual models with an above-chance level. What is not clear in these studies, however, is whether the subjects had prior exposure—even on a minimal basis—to pictorial material, and evidence of this nature is crucial for an understanding of how the ability to process information presented in these modalities develops. (See R. J. Miller, in press, for a thorough review of this line of work.)

While there may be some amount of object recognition in simplified presentations, there is no doubt that the kind of pictorial material that is common in modern nations—such as the photographs with which we introduced this section—presents great difficulties to many traditional peoples. An ingenious line of research initiated several years ago by Hudson has helped us to understand some of the factors at work, particularly the role of Western conventions of perspective in pictorial representation.

Hudson (1962b) was concerned with a practical problem: how to train largely nonliterate Bantu workers employed in South African mines and factories. He found that training films and safety posters often failed to have the desired effect, and an investigation indicated that the problem was one of interpretation— the visually presented material was being misinterpreted or not interpreted at all.

In order to make a systematic investigation of the factors involved, Hudson employed a set of cards, some of which are shown in Figure 4–3.

All of the pictures contain figures of an elephant, an antelope, and a man pointing a spear. In each picture the spear is aligned with both the elephant and the antelope. The subject is asked various questions designed to elicit what he sees in the picture. Most important for assessing the use of depth cues is a question like "What is the man doing with the spear?" and if this fails to yield a response, "Which animal is the man aiming the spear at?"

The pictures differ with respect to the cues available for interpreting the picture. Cards 1 and 2 contain the depth cues of object

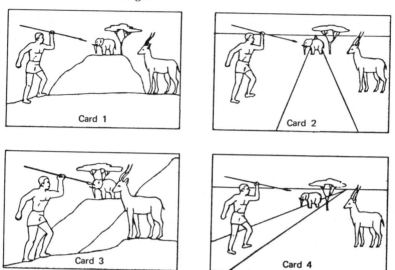

Figure 4-3. Pictures for study of depth perception in Africa.

size and superposition; cards 3 and 4 contain perspective cues as well.

Materials such as these were used with several different groups of people in South Africa (Hudson, 1962a, b) and Ghana (Mundy-Castle, 1966). Among the groups studied were European and Bantu primary school children of various ages, Bantu secondary school children, nonliterate European and Bantu workers, and Indian school children. Results showed that at the beginning of primary school, the European children had a great deal of trouble perceiving the pictures as three-dimensional—that is, they would say that the man was aiming his spear at the elephant. By the end of primary school, virtually all these children responded to the stimuli as three-dimensional. Not so the Bantu children (in Hudson's sample) or the Ghanian children (in Mundy-Castle's sample). These children all tended to interpret the pictures in a two-dimensional fashion. Hudson also found that the nonliterate laborers, both Bantu and European, and Indian children responded to the pictures as flat, rather than three-dimensional. He concludes from this set of studies that

> formal schooling in the normal course is not the principal determinant in pictorial perception. Informal instruction in the home and habitual exposure to pictures play a much larger role (1967, p. 95).

This conclusion is seconded by Mundy-Castle, who also conducted surveys in the communities and homes of the children who participated in his experiment. He reports that he found

> no evidence of activities such as reading, drawing, painting, looking at pictures, pattern-making, or playing with constructional toys, and it was exceptional for a child to have used a pencil prior to going to school. . . . The opportunity for informal pictorial experience was therefore negligible (1966, p. 298).

These results seem quite convincing for Hudson's task. But how representative is the task itself? Is it the case that people who respond inappropriately to questions about Hudson's pictures simply can't perceive pictures three-dimensionally? Or are there other ways of evaluating what people see, perhaps with different kinds of stimuli, that would reveal three-dimensional perceptions?

This is the question asked by Deregowski (1968b), who has carried out many studies on the relation between culture and perception. His work was conducted with 7- to 16-year-old schoolboys (average years in school, 3.9) and adult domestic workers in the city of Lusaka, Zambia.

To each subject Deregowski gave a version of Hudson's test, using pictures like those in Figure 4–3. Then he presented subjects with quite different kinds of pictures, shown in Figure 4–4. Instead of asking subjects questions about these pictures, Deregowski asked them to construct a model of the picture, using sticks that could be stuck together easily. Of course, he made sure that each person knew how to make a model with the sticks in a practice session.

The major question was, would people who respond two-dimensionally when asked about Hudson's pictures also respond two-dimensionally when asked to make models of abstract line drawings? In general, Deregowski's answer to this question was *no*.

Consistent with previous results, Deregowski found that verbal statements about the object relationships portrayed in Hudson's pictures overwhelmingly indicated two-dimensional perception: 100 percent of the domestic workers and 80 percent of the schoolboys responded in this manner. *But more than half of these same subjects constructed three-dimensional models of the figures in*

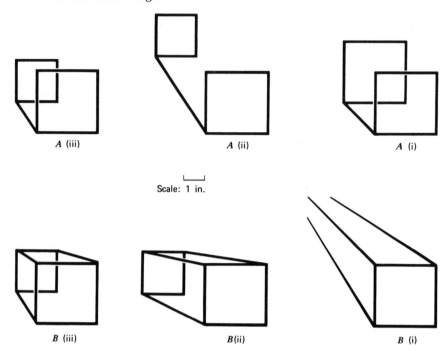

Figure 4-4. Drawings used for construction models in depth perception test.

Deregowski's pictures! The models were not always perfect, but they clearly reflected information about depth. Deregowski summarizes these results in the following manner:

> The frequency with which subjects who were 2D on Hudson's test made 3D responses to the construction test suggests that it is probably illegitimate to extrapolate from Hudson's findings to all types of pictorial material. A subject, it appears, cannot be classified as a 2D perceiver of all pictorial material merely because he is a 2D perceiver as far as Hudson's test is concerned. This does not invalidate Hudson's remarks about the difficulties which might arise owing to the cross-cultural differences in pictorial perception (Hudson, 1960, 1962a, b). It *does*, however, limit their applicability by excluding, at least in part, the type of pictorial material used in the construction test (Deregowski, 1968b, p. 203).

This work clearly demonstrates that we cannot talk glibly about 2-D and 3-D perceivers as if they were different people. But it is not clear what gets a person to respond three-dimensionally under some circumstances and two-dimensionally under others.

Deregowski emphasizes that the content of the picture is important. But we also ought to consider the influence of what kind of response subjects are asked to make. It might well be that what someone is asked to do with a picture influences his attention to particular cues; the request to make a stick model certainly is not the same as asking questions about a hunter's target. What would have happened, for example, if subjects had been shown a three-dimensional board-model of the contents of Hudson's pictures and asked to place the hunter and the antelope (or the hunter, the antelope, and the elephant) in their correct positions? If this construction task influences the expression of three-dimensional responses, a new dimension would be added to the study of pictorial depth perception. If it does not, we would confidently narrow our study of factors influencing three-dimensional pictorial perception to the questions of picture *content*, emphasized by Deregowski.

Several other experimental observations point strongly to the influence of culturally patterned conventions on the perception of pictorial material. Hudson reports several studies in which various pictorial conventions taken for granted by Europeans were absent in tribal Africans. Among these was the use of foreshortening to indicate perspective: a picture of a man ascending stairs was seen appropriately by literate European children, but nonliterate African children saw the man as maimed, one leg being shorter than the other. African students asked to draw a cow in profile showed all four cloven hooves, two horns, and two ears, much as if the pupils were making a combination of profile and frontal views, while European students drew a profile. Hudson concludes that the European child draws what he sees, literally, even though he knows it may be conceptually inaccurate, while the African draws what he knows to be there—a cow is not a cow without four cloven hooves.

Perception of Orientation

Another convention that we take for granted, but which is almost certainly learned, is the orientation and positioning of a figure on a sheet of paper. In Western art, objects are normally positioned with reference to the base of the page and its sides: African children studied by Hudson drew all over their pages and the orientation of each figure was, to all intents and purposes, random.

This latter finding raises an interesting question: Do nonliterate people experience actual difficulty in *perceiving* the orientation of objects in pictures, or do they simply ignore our conventions when asked to reproduce a picture?

Deregowski (1968c) posed the question as follows: In perceiving the orientation of one depicted object relative to another, does difficulty arise from the angle at which the picture was taken (he used photographs) or from the subject's position when he is asked to reconstruct a pictorial arrangement? He also wanted to determine whether subjects would be influenced by the contents of the depicted scene.

In a study of 11-year-old schoolchildren in Lusaka, Zambia, he used the apparatus shown in Figure 4–5. This figure is a schematic drawing of a board with a toy Land Rover in the center. In the first of two studies, the Land Rover was alone on the board. In

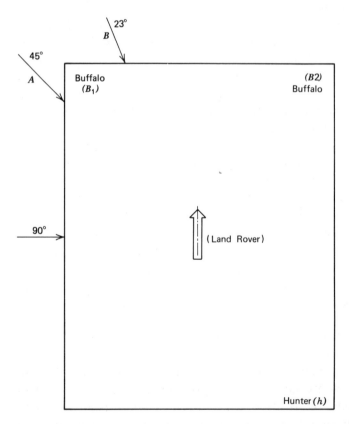

Figure 4-5. Arrangement of objects in Zambian study of pictorial orientation.

the second there were toy buffalos at C1 and C2 as well as a hunter at H. The hunter was pointing his gun at buffalo number 2.

For Experiment 1 there were three photographs of the Land Rover taken from just above ground level. The photographs were taken from the angles indicated by the arrows at 23°, 45°, and 90°, and from such a distance that the truck was seen to be in the middle of the board.

For the reproduction trials, in which the subject had to position the truck to accord with its location in a photograph, the Land Rover was mounted on a freely rotating disc in the center of the board, and the board was placed on the floor. Each subject was shown a picture taken from one of the three angles and asked to place the truck just as it appeared in the picture. Different groups of subjects stood at different angles to the truck (23°, 45°, or 90°).

The main question was to determine whether subjects misjudged orientation, and how.

Deregowski's results show that his subjects certainly did make errors in their judgment of orientation of the Land Rover: if the camera angle and the subjects's viewing angle coincided, placement was more or less accurate. But when camera and subject viewing angles did *not* coincide, gross errors occurred. Deregowski summarizes the pattern of responses as reflecting a process whereby the subjects assume that the camera occupied the position that they, at the moment, occupy and hence make adjustments in which the car is at approximately the same angle to themselves as it is to the camera (1968c, pp. 152–153).

In Experiment 2, Deregowski sought to determine whether the content of the photographs would influence the subjects' perceptions of orientation.

For this purpose, he used the two toy buffalos and the hunter, but removed the Land Rover. He then photographed three arrangements of buffalo and hunter. In the first picture, both buffalos were present; in the second, only buffalo 1 was present; in the third, only buffalo 2 was present. The hunter always aimed at the spot where buffalo 2 was supposed to be placed, *even when that buffalo was absent.*

The question then became, would subjects who are asked to place the toy hunter in the same position as the photographed hunter reorient him to make the scene realistic? That is, would they make the hunter point at buffalo 1 if buffalo 2 were absent? Subjects did change their responses to the different displays in the way predicted if they were trying to make the reproduction sensible. Moreover, when Deregowski compared the results for different camera angles in Experiment 2 with the size of errors he had obtained in Experiment 1, he found that the subjects seemed to be more influenced by their desire to render a meaningful reproduction than by camera angle.

Although other research along the same general lines could be cited, it is clear that pictorial representation and the interpretation of pictorial material have a large experiential component to them, which involves the mastery of conventionalized forms of representation and conventionalized definitions of the task (such as making a distinction between what one "sees" and what one "knows," for example).

An important question that remains to be clarified is to what extent such perceptual habits acquired early in life are reversible later. Even college-educated Africans often interpreted Hudson's pictures two-dimensionally, and so did most of the schoolboys in Deregowski's study. But Dawson (1967) reported that three-dimensional interpretations can be taught rather easily.

He selected 24 young Temne mine apprentices who in an earlier study had given two-dimensional responses when shown drawings using depth cues. From this population, he set up two groups matched in education (all were in secondary school), in intelligence test scores, and in other characteristics in which he was interested. The training group received 8 hours of instruction in drawing pictures with depth cues; the others acted as controls. Both groups were retested three months later to see whether training effects, if present, would endure over time. The training group showed significant improvement in the use of 3-D cues, as compared with the control group when retested on the original material as well as on new material. These results suggest that specific instruction in the conventions of pictorial representation rather than general exposure to pictorial material may be the critical learning experience for 3-D responses, but one training study confined to one population is inadequate evidence; this is clearly an important question for future research.

Visual Illusions

One way to study the influence of past experiences on perception is to set up an experimental situation where the normally useful cues are misleading. Therefore, the study of visual illusions has provided interesting evidence of the relation between culture and perception.

Segall, Campbell, and Herskovits (1966) conducted the first systematic study of perceptual illusions across cultures. They also provide a lucid and comprehensive discussion of the rationale and methods needed to make such studies successful. Although their particular theory can no longer be considered adequate, their method of approach is a good starting point for a discussion of this problem.

They worked with two well-known visual illusions, the Muller-Lyer illusion and the horizontal-vertical illusion (see Figure 4–6), asking members of many different cultural groups to respond to these two perceptual stimuli. They reasoned that if different groups of people raised in different environments had different inferential habits when it came to using such cues as distance and length, these groups ought to respond differently to illusory stimuli.

In particular, Segall and his associates hypothesized that people growing up in Western environments, which they characterize as *carpentered* (with regular rectangular objects, straight lines, and

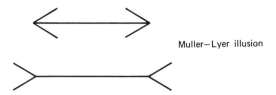

Muller—Lyer illusion

Are the two horizontal sections the same length?

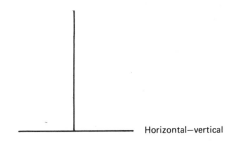

Horizontal—vertical

Are the vertical and horizontal segments the same length?

Figure 4-6. Visual illusions used in Segall, Campbell, and Herskovits cross-cultural study.

so forth), would tend to be more subject to the Muller-Lyer illusion than people who have not been exposed to such regular geometric relationships; similarly, the horizontal-vertical illusion would be weaker in people whose environments provide little opportunity to view the horizon or to see great distances (such as jungle dwellers) and stronger in people whose environments required them to make many such distance perceptions.

The researchers took many precautions to make sure that their subjects understood the task and that the experimental procedures were the same from sample to sample. The subject had only to indicate which of two lines was longer each time he was shown a stimulus pair. Many different examples of each of the illusory stimuli, as well as stimuli that did not produce any illusion, were presented to each subject. When the data had been collected, it was possible to get a score for each subject, indicating the extent of his susceptibility to the illusion.

This experiment was conducted with almost 2000 people from 14 non-European locations and the United States. The results showed that American subjects were more susceptible to the Muller-Lyer illusion and that many, but not all, of the non-European groups were more susceptible to the horizontal-vertical illusion. Segall and associates concluded that response to these illusions varies with the conditions of an individual's (or group's) environment: carpentered environments lead to misperception of the Muller-Lyer figures and experience with long, uninterrupted views enhances susceptibility to the horizontal-vertical illusion. (Note, however, that illusion-supported responses were found in all the cultures studied; that is, the illusions *were*, to a lesser or greater extent, illusions.)

The story of research on cultural-environmental effects and susceptibility to illusions does not stop here. As so often happens in scientific research, a particular fact may have more than one interpretation, and this is very much the case with the findings just reported.

One alternative explanation is provided by Gustav Jahoda (1966). He conducted the same experiment, using the same materials, with two groups of Ghanaian subjects and a group of Europeans. The two Ghanaian groups were from different parts of Ghana, and one of the groups had adopted more Westernized, "carpentered" technology. This would lead us to predict, on the basis of the *carpen-*

tered world hypothesis that the Westernized Ghanaian group and the European group would respond alike, but differently from the non-westernized Ghanaian group. However, the two Ghanaian groups responded alike and were less susceptible to the Muller-Lyer illusion than the European group. Jahoda concluded that some factor other than carpenteredness of the environment must account for the data. He suggested that the explanation might lie in the difficulty all Ghanaian subjects have in interpreting pictorial material.

More recent attempts to account for variations in susceptibility to the Muller-Lyer illusion across different human groups implicate physiological as well as cultural and ecological factors. This work stems from Pollack's discovery (Pollack, 1970; Pollack and Silvar, 1967) of a strong relation between a specific property of the visual system—retinal pigmentation—and susceptibility to this illusion: the more dense the pigmentation, the less the illusion susceptibility. Since it is generally known that retinal pigmentation is more dense among dark-skinned people, Pollack compared the susceptibility to the illusion of dark- and light-skinned children in the United States and found, as expected, that the dark-skinned children were less susceptible.

Could this relationship account for the cross-cultural results? Berry (1971a), who has studied the Muller-Lyer illusion in a variety of cultures, originally thought that he had supported the carpentered world hypothesis when he had found a significant correlation between this ecological factor and extent of illusion. But when he reanalyzed his data, he found that degree of pigmentation was more highly correlated with susceptibility to the illusion than was carpenteredness. However, Jahoda (1971) questions the *ad hoc* ranking of skin color for Scottish, African, Eskimo, Australian aboriginal, and New Guinea Melanesian communities; the "actual values of the correlations should be regarded with some reservation," he says (p. 200).

In a carefully designed study, Jahoda tested other hypotheses derived from Pollack, suggesting that for individuals with dense retinal pigmentation susceptibility to the illusion should vary, depending on whether a figure is drawn in red or in blue, whereas individuals with less dense pigmentation should do about the same with either color. With populations of African and Scottish students, Jahoda did, indeed, find that the African, but not the Scottish, students performed differently on the red and blue stimulus figures. While this confirmed certain aspects of Pollack's theory, an interesting feature of the results was that overall illusion susceptibility was somewhat higher among the Africans—a reversal of the original findings by Segall's group, which set off the theorizing in the first place! Jahoda concludes, "it seems likely from these and other studies that no single factor can adequately account for the observed variations in M-L illusion susceptibility" (p. 206).

Bornstein (1973) used the pigmentation hypothesis to make predictions about how cultures in the original study made by Segall's group would rank on Muller-Lyer illusion susceptibility. The rank ordering predicted by pigmentation data fit Segall's obtained results quite nicely. In an interesting extension of this line of reasoning, Bornstein went on to develop the notion that differences in pigmentation associated with differences in sensitivity to certain colors (especially those in the blue-green range of the color spectrum) might account for cultural differences in primary color names. A survey of color names in 126 societies showed a regular geographic patterning of color naming that did indeed parallel the distribution of eye pigmentation. These data have fascinating implications for two of the most controversial issues in cross-cultural research. For one thing, they raise the possibility that people in different cultures may, in fact, *see* color differently. Secondly, they suggest that the relation between perceptual and linguistic phenomena in the color domain may be the very reverse of that posited by Whorf—color *vocabulary* may be determined by color *vision.*

Bornstein's careful work relates the physiological characteristic of yellow ocular pigmentation to environmental variations (differences in exposure to ultraviolet rays, which vary with altitude and proximity to the equator) and differences in diet. Thus, environmental differences operating through *physiological* mechanisms might contribute substantially to the two classical cognitive phenomena (color naming and susceptibility to visual illusions) for which evidence of differences among people is strongest. Discussing the deficiencies of earlier single-factor explanations of these phenomena, Bornstein says that his psychophysiological approach is not offered as the sole explanation of cultural differences. "Most probably," he points out, "the interactional complexity of environment, culture, and organism will disallow any monistic view" (p. 43).

This line of work is an important reminder that specific physiological characteristics of receptor systems need to be taken into account in perceptual research, and that when physiological and cultural factors co-vary, it is folly to pursue one without taking account of the other.

Another example of differential responses to illusions comes from a study of the Zulu of Natal made by Allport and Pettigrew (1957). Their experiment made use of the rotating trapezoidal window illusion (see Figure 4–7). The window is so proportioned that when it rotates, the length of the longer edge is always longer on the retina than the shorter edge. The perception normally reported is that the window appears to be swaying back and forth instead of rotating. The explanation given by the inventor of the illusion (Ames, 1951) is that the observer, familiar with *rectangular* windows, assumes that this window, too, is rectangular. From long practice in viewing objects of all types the subject interprets the window as oscillating rather than rotating.

Allport and Pettigrew studied Zulu responses to the trapezoi-

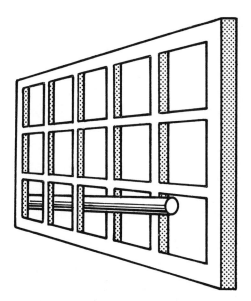

Figure 4-7. Apparatus for studying trapezoidal window illusion (adapted from British Psychological Society).

dal windows because they hypothesized that traditional Zulu culture "is probably the most spherical or circular of all Bantu cultures, possibly the most spherical of all native African cultures."
Round rather than angular style is the aesthetic ideal; huts, corrals,
fields, doorways, and many other aspects of the Zulu cultural environment are round where Europeans would expect to find angular shapes prevailing. The Zulu language has a word for round,
but none for square.

The experiment was conducted with four groups: rural African
boys from two different areas, a group of urban African boys, and
a group of urban European boys. Testing for the illusion was carried out under four conditions, varying from easy to difficult.

Previous research in the United States had shown that the *more
difficult* the viewing conditions, the *more likely* it was that subjects would be fooled by the illusion. In South Africa, Allport and
Pettigrew found also that all groups reported the illusion under
difficult viewing conditions. But under the easiest viewing conditions, the Westernized groups reported more illusory responses
than the traditional groups. The authors conclude that *both* an
effect of culture on perception *and* evidence for general-human
perceptual processes are suggested by the pattern of results: the
general-human process is manifested under difficult viewing conditions, the cultural influence under easy viewing conditions. Under
the easy viewing conditions the fact that Westerners and Wester-
ized Zulus live in a carpentered environment, with many examples
of right angles and rectangular windows, leads them to make the
wrong inferences even under conditions where the traditional
Zulus stop being influenced by the illusion and report correctly
on the motion of the window.

Perception and Attention: The Problem of Selection

Thus far we have emphasized the way in which a person's experience, or lack of experience, with certain phenomena may affect
the way he organizes stimulus information (as in perception of
pictorial representations and illusions). In this section, we will inquire about cultural influences on the *selective* aspects of perception. We are constantly bombarded by a barrage of stimuli, but at
any one time we attend to only a small set of this available stimu-

lation. Does cultural experience affect perception by guiding the selection process?

Binocular Rivalry

One way to approach the problem of selection is to take advantage of the phenomenon of binocular rivalry: When two different objects are shown to a subject, and each object is seen with a different eye, subjects usually report that they see one object first and then the other. Sometimes, if the objects are similar, the pictures "fuse" and the subject reports seeing a single object combining features of the two.

Berry (1969) used this technique to determine whether familiarity, in the sense of cultural relevance, would influence what subjects tend to see first. As part of a larger study of the relation between culture and perception, he tested Eskimos and subjects from Sierra Leone, West Africa (Temne), using photographs of five pairs of objects. One member of each pair was an object familiar to the Temne, the other a corresponding object familiar to the Eskimo. The object-pairs (for example, man-man or house-house) were shown twice to each subject so that each picture could be shown to each eye. Berry also made sure to check each person's vision. The results were consistent with the idea that culture would influence what a person saw when conflicting pictures were presented to his two eyes: a greater number of the culturally familiar pictures were seen first.

Many questions come to mind concerning these interesting findings. For example, did the subjects really "see" the more familiar item sooner, or did they just report it first? Could cultural relevance and frequency be separated as factors influencing the results? For example, would Eskimos see a Temne man more quickly than some rare, but relevant, feature of Eskimo society? These questions notwithstanding, Berry's work clearly indicates that subjects are predisposed to attend to and report things with which they are familiar, and the questions we raise are certainly answerable through further research.

Perceptual-Cognitive Styles

Berry's work on culture and selective perception was carried out within a general framework that Witkin (1967) calls a *cogni-*

tive style theory. The term *cognitive style* refers to modes of functioning that characterize an individual's perceptual and intellectual activities. Extensive research by Witkin and his associates shows that people tend to be consistent in the way they approach tasks requiring cognitive skills, just as they are likely to be consistent in the attitudes and emotions they bring to situations. Although there is a wide diversity of individual styles, Witkin found they could be ordered along a dimension he calls *global–articulated*. A person with an *articulated* cognitive style is one who is skilled at differentiating and organizing features of the environment and at distinguishing between phenomena that are internal to his self and those external to it. A *global* style is the opposite.

Although Witkin applies his theory very widely, most cross-cultural research has concentrated on differences in *perceptual* style. In the area of perception, the terms *field-dependence* and *field-independence* are used to designate the two major cognitive styles, global and articulated, respectively. An intuitive idea of what is meant by these terms can be grasped by an examination of Figure 4–8. This is an example of an item in the *embedded figure test*, which is widely used to diagnose perceptual styles. The subject is first shown a picture of the small triangle on the left and is then shown the complex geometric figure on the right. The question is: Will he be able to break up or analyze the complex figure to find the simple one, and how long will it take him to do it? The person who performs accurately and quickly on this test is considered to be field-independent.

Witkin's theory is relevant to the study of culture and perception because he believes that there is a normal course of cognitive development from the global end of the spectrum to the artic-

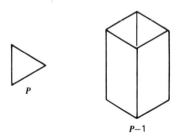

Figure 4-8. Type of stimulus material used to study perception of embedded figures.

ulated end (compare Werner, 1961). The young child does not clearly differentiate himself from his environment, but as he grows he becomes aware of the boundaries of his body and personality and gains a sense of separate identity. This process of psychological differentiation is reflected in his cognitive and perceptual styles.

According to Witkin both sociocultural and environmental factors influence the course of psychological differentiation. The two sociocultural influences he discusses are (1) the opportunity given the child to achieve separation, or independence, particularly in his family situation and principally by his mother, and (2) the way in which adults treat the child's expression of impulse: differentiation is fostered when the child is permitted to form his own standards of behavior and has to deal with his own impulses. The most important environmental factor is the degree to which the environment is variegated and contains a lot of what Witkin calls "structure," as contrasted with one that is homogeneous and gives very few structural cues.

Examples of the way these ideas have been applied to the question of cultural differences in perception come from the work of Dawson (1967) and Berry (1966; 1971b).

Dawson worked with two tribal groups, the Temne and the Mende in Sierra Leone, West Africa. These groups were said to contrast sharply with respect to "tribal values, severity of child-rearing practices, and other socialization practices" (p. 122).

> Temne tribal values are much more aggressive than the western-type values of the Mende. The Temne mother is extremely dominating whilst discipline in the Temne home is very strict. . . . [T]he Mende people have much less severe socialization processes, the Mende mother is not as dominating, and individual initiative is encouraged to a greater extent than occurs with the Temne (p. 122).

In view of what has been said about Witkin's theory, these differences in child-rearing practices lead to the prediction that the Temne will be less articulated, more field-dependent, than the Mende because Mende early experiences have been such as to foster differentiation, while Temne experiences do not. As measured by a specially prepared version of the embedded figures test, this hypothesis received support in Dawson's study; the Mende showed significantly higher scores for articulated functioning on this test.

Berry (1966) extended this analysis to include differences in the nature of the physical environment as well as differences in socio-cultural factors having to do with early childhood. One of the cultures studied was Temne (already described in connection with Dawson's work); the comparison culture was a Canadian Eskimo culture. Both traditional and transitional groups were drawn from each culture. A group was called transitional if its members had become involved in Western-style economic enterprises and lived in Western-style housing. Berry reports that the Eskimos treat their children with great kindness and rarely punish them. Considerable freedom is given the children, who are expected to develop independent skills. Berry's description of the Temne is very much like Dawson's. He adds that there is a strong ethic to conform in Temne society, fostered by secret societies and very harsh discipline after the child reaches the age of two and a half years. These factors would lead us to expect more field-dependence and less articulation in the Temne than in the Eskimos.

In addition to the contrast in their child-rearing practices, the Temne and Eskimo obviously can be contrasted with respect to the visual aspects of their environments. The Temne landscape is covered with tropical vegetation; varieties of color and contour in the rich green jungle growth, in the abundant flowers, in streams and rivers. The Eskimo environment appears barren to us at any time of the year. In winter, virtually all is white. In the summer, which lasts only a few weeks, moss and lichen cover the rocky landscape giving the area a grey-brown tone. Berry considers the Eskimo landscape to represent a homogenous, unstructured environment and the Temne landscape a variegated, structured one. By comparison with the Temne, whose livelihood depends mostly on farming, the Eskimo hunter must be skilled at picking out seemingly minor variations in his homogeneous view, and he must be able to navigate freely in a relatively featureless environment in search of game. Thus, environmental as well as cultural factors predict greater differentiation and less field-dependence among the Eskimo.

Consistent with this analysis and Witkin's theory, Berry finds that in contrast to the Temne, the Eskimo are very field-independent (differentiated) as measured by the embedded figures and other tests. Their performance is similar to a comparison group of Scottish subjects. The Temne were considerably more field-dependent than either the Eskimo or Scottish groups. Other results also fit with Berry's analysis of the difference between Eskimo and Temne environments. For instance, in a task of reproducing pictures that contained figures with slight discontinuities in them (geometric figures with a small gap at some point) the Eskimos were more sensitive to the gap than the Temne. Also significant is the fact that the more Westernized groups among both the Temne and the Eskimo tested higher than the traditional groups on these perceptual skills. Berry concludes

> that ecological demands and cultural practices are significantly related to the development of perceptual skills. . . . In some sense, cultural and psychological development are congruent; cultural characteristics allow people to develop and maintain those skills which they have to (1967, p. 228).

He makes two other points that are of general relevance to this discussion. (1) In view of minimal differences between the Scottish and Eskimo samples (in contrast with the Temne) and the significant differences between traditional and transitional groups within each culture, explanation of the differences in terms of racial factors is very unconvincing; and (2) The great Temne–Eskimo differences should caution us not to lump all primitive, non-Western peoples together "as if they were cognitively homogeneous."

As important and valid as these two last points are, we must be very cautious in trying to interpret the specific results reported by Berry. The distinction we need to make here will recur often in our later discussion of cultural differences in problem solving and other learning tasks. Berry makes a plausible case for the theoretical account of his cultural-perceptual differences, but as he himself points out, it is not possible to separate sociocultural and environmental effects in these studies because hypothetically both operate in the same direction; on either sociocultural grounds (child-rearing practices) *or* environmental grounds (uniform versus varied perceptual environments) Berry would predict greater differentiation and field-independence for the Eskimo. As matters stand, we can not locate the source of the difference.

Moreover, we might well ask whether the Temne jungle environment is really more structured than the Eskimo arctic environment. Is it any less of an isolating skill to be able to spot a camouflaged deer hiding in a jungle thicket than to spot a polar bear on an ice floe? Isn't the Temne jungle environment, in fact, more like the example of the embedded figures test given in Figure 4–8? The Temne hunter, too, must be able to find his way around in an environment that is, to the naive observer, "featureless." Presumably, a critical difference, from Berry's point of view, is that the Eskimo *must* hunt to live, while the Temne spend most of their time farming and rarely have to depend on fine perceptual judgments.

The fact that we raise these questions does not mean that we consider Berry's research to be of poor quality. Instead we need to emphasize that the manifestation of every cognitive skill is determined by many factors. In order to pinpoint which factor (or factors) may be at work, several experiments are almost surely required. It will also be necessary to find some adequate way to characterize environments (jungle versus arctic is probably too global a description for detailed research). What is more, the characterizations must be consistent and independent of the test we are interested in; otherwise we may find ourselves making up different descriptions of the same environment to fit any new result that comes along.

Berry was quite aware of these difficulties, and in subsequent work he set out to deal with them. The first requirement was to get away from the two-culture comparison by adding several more cultural samples to his study. This he did by working with four cultures, all of which had subsistence-level economies. Within each culture, two subgroups were chosen; one of the subgroups lived in a style that was as close as could be found to traditional patterns, in rural areas, while the other had a transitional life style and lived in an urban setting.

Berry (1971b) summarized his argument as follows:

> Hunting peoples are expected to possess good visual discrimination and spatial skill, and their cultures are expected to be supportive of the development of these skills through the presence of a high number of "geometrical spatial" concepts, a highly developed and generally shared arts and crafts production, and socialization practices whose content emphasizes independence and self reliance, and whose techniques are supportive and encouraging of separate development. Implicit in this argument is the expectation that as hunting diminishes in importance across samples ranked in terms of this ecology dimension, the discrimination and spatial

skills will diminish, as will each of the three cultural aids (1971b, p. 328).

Note that Berry is hypothesizing a link between the ecological demands on a group and socialization practices. To test these ideas, Berry gave four tasks to samples of subjects in each cultural subgroup: a test of ability to make fine discriminations and three "tests of spatial skill," including the embedded figures test. The groups were from several areas of the world: the Temne of Sierra Leone, New Guinea natives, Australian aborigines, and Eskimos.

The results of this large study were generally consistent with Berry's hypothesis, although he found that *education*, as a special institution, had to be taken into consideration.

When his four cultural groups were ranked according to the importance of hunting, he found that improvements in discrimination ability and performance on the three spatial tests paralleled the increase in hunting requirements. A special influence of education was hypothesized because the transitional-urban samples generally performed better than the corresponding traditional-rural groups.

Consistent with his earlier findings on the Temne and Eskimo, Berry found that severity of child-rearing practices and emphasis on conformity decreased as hunting became more important. These results and others led Berry to conclude:

> It is apparent from the data that the visual skills are developed to a degree predictable from an analysis of the ecological demands facing the group, and the cultural aids developed by them. Further it is apparent that there are relationships between the ecological and psychological variables which are more than dichotomized ones; they appear to covary in a systematic way (cf. weak version of ecological-behavioural interaction) and can be demonstrated to be adaptive to the ecological demands placed on the group (cf. moderate version of ecological-behavioural interaction). Finally the psychological underpinnings of technological development, often isolated as spatial ability, are shown to develop in relation to an ecology, which by way of technological change is open to change itself (1971b, p. 335).

We can certainly agree that Berry has identified an orderly relation between cultural-environmental variables on the one hand and psychological skills on the other. Inclusion of degrees of cultural-environmental differences greatly increases the plausibility of his explanations. Such inclusive studies are all too rare in this area of research.

There are still many remaining questions about the relation between ecology and psychological processes, even those processes studied by Berry. One problem is that Berry's use of the term *ecology* is too broad. Hunting, for example, is an *activity*—what people do in their ecology. It might well be that it is not hunting but some other aspect of these people's lives that accounts for the patterns of performance we have been discussing. For example, we might expect that if hunting experience is of critical importance, we would see a difference in spatial skills between hunters and nonhunters within a society that emphasizes hunting. One way to test this notion is to compare men's and women's performances among the Eskimos and Aborigines, Berry's two hunting samples. Surprisingly, no significant sex differences in test performance occur in these societies, although the women are not hunters in either of them. This raises once again the problem of isolating causal factors when several variables (hunting practices, socialization patterns) co-vary.

A quite different set of problems was raised by Wober (1967) working in Nigeria. Wober gave his subjects two tests of field-dependence, the embedded figures test used by Dawson and Berry, and a rod and frame test, which has also been used in this kind of research in the United States.

In the rod and frame test the subject sits in a dark room and looks at a display consisting of a luminous square frame with a luminous rod mounted in the center of it. Both the rod and the frame can be tilted at any angle relative to the ground. The chair in which the subject sits can also be tilted, and, as a result, a new set of cues, in addition to visual ones, enters the picture. These are *proprioceptive* cues—internal bodily sensations. Since the chair comes equipped with a footrest that tips along with the rest of the chair, the subject cannot make physical contact with the floor. This means that when the chair is tilted, the subject has to use cues that he receives from his own body in response to the force of gravity—cues from his muscles and his inner ear—to tell him where he is. This experiment studies the effects of both visual and proprioceptive cues.

The subject's task is to set the rod to a *vertical position* with respect to the ground. Insofar as he is able to do this, he is said to be independent of the individual and proprioceptive stimuli that might mislead him.

A situation that might confront a subject in this test is shown in Figure 4–9.

Wober conducted this study with 86 men from southern Nigeria, all of whom worked for a large company and some of whom were educated, to various degrees. The major results are presented in two parts.

First, Wober calculated the errors in rod adjustment when the person was tilted but the frame was not. Errors here would presumably reflect errors in responding to the proprioceptive cues that indicate the amount of body tilt. Under these conditions, American subjects made errors that averaged about 3.5 degrees, while the Nigerian errors averaged only 1.25 degrees. When the frame and body were both tilted, the problem was more difficult. Under these conditions, subjects from both cultures made larger errors, but there were no reliable differences between the Nigerians' scores and those of the Americans. In only one case did the Americans make smaller errors. This occurred when the frame

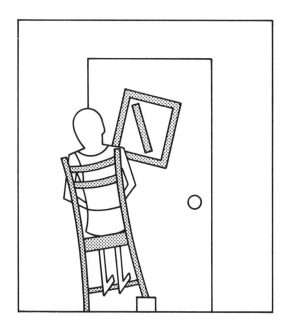

Figure 4-9. Rod-and-frame test (adapted from British Psychological Society).

was tilted but the person was not. In this case the Africans' errors were about as great as when they themselves were tilted, but American errors were only half as large. This is exactly what we would expect if the African subjects found it more difficult to make judgments based on visual cues than on proprioceptive ones.

The other major finding in this study was the absence of a correlation between performance on the rod and frame test and performance on the embedded figures test; the two tests did not seem to reflect a single, underlying psychological process. These results do not in any way contradict Berry and Dawson's findings. Rather, they suggest, as did Deregowski's work on making models from three-dimensional pictures, that findings obtained with one test instrument do not necessarily reflect the workings of a general psychological mechanism.

Wober's conclusions are very much to the point.

> It would appear that "style of cognitive functioning" is not so uniform throughout all fields of an individual's expression as had originally been supposed by Witkin. The finding in America that the [embedded frames test] and similar visual tests indicated a person's level of psychological differentiation was supported in Sierra Leone . . . using visual tests. However, visual tests do not appear to be the sole indicators of psychological differentiation. The evidence here is that such differentiation may occur in sensory fields other than the visual one (p. 37).

Wober goes on to suggest that the expression of differentiation probably depends on early experience that emphasizes the visual or proprioceptive modes. This suggestion would certainly be interesting to test; if Wober had been able to work with Berry's different cultural groups, he would perhaps have found that as hunting activity increases in importance, dancing and other "proprioception skills" decrease!

Attribute Preference: Color, Form, Number, and Size

Another experimental setting used to study how subjects selectively respond to environmental stimuli focuses on preferences for particular stimulus attributes. For example, a sizable literature has grown up around preferences when the materials used as stimuli vary along such dimensions as color, form, size, number, and function. Normal American children exhibit orderly developmental trends in their preferences for certain of these dimensions.

The conventional wisdom about color-or-form preference, which is supported by a good deal of evidence from European and American children aged 2 to 8 years, is that younger children prefer color to form, but that some time during the fourth year form comes to be preferred. Typical is an experiment by Suchman and Trabasso (1966) in which children aged 3 to 6 years were presented with slides such as those shown in Figure 4–10 and asked to "point to the two that are the same." Children up to 4 years of age chose to match on the basis of color, rather than form; most older children matched on form.

This change from color to form preference is accompanied by

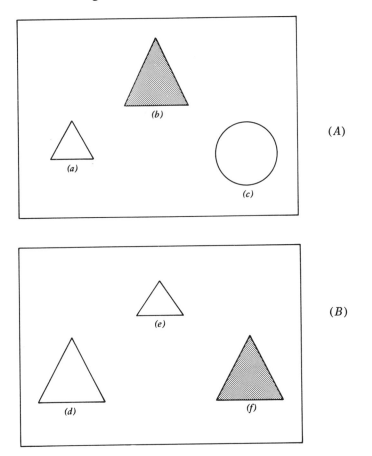

Figure 4-10. (A) Card for testing dimensional preference where color, form, and size vary. Items *a* and *b* are the same form; *a* and *c* are the same color; *b* and *c* are the same size.
(B) Card for testing dimensional preference where one dimension (form) is excluded. Items *d* and *e* are the same color; Items *d* and *f* are the same size.

changes in other cognitive spheres. Children who prefer form have higher mental test scores, and perform better on a variety of classification and concept-formation tasks than do children who prefer color.

These trends are interesting when considered in cross-cultural perspective because it is found that African tribal children do *not* show the developmental trend characteristic of European children. Suchman (1966) worked with Yoruba children attending a Koranic school in Nigeria. She found that at all of the ages studied (3 to 15), children preferred color to form, with no age trends. Serpell (1969) obtained similar results with Zambian tribal children, but his data go a little further in explaining the factors controlling color–form preferences. He found that children attending certain schools did show an age-related increase in perference for form over color and that university students had a strong perference for form, while illiterate adults preferred color to form. Even very young Zambians showed a form preference if they attended an elite school in Zambia's capital city, but, interestingly, other schoolchildren did not. Serpell accounts for these results (as well as analogous results with American deaf people) by what he calls the *perceptual experience* hypothesis: It is assumed that initially all children prefer color and that the shift to form preference is caused by the guided play that goes on in the typical middle-class European home or in Western schools; for school performance, forms are clearly more important attributes of things than colors (in reading, for instance). Otherwise there is no reason why a subject should choose form on logical grounds. Presumably the failure of certain school situations to produce the shift from color to form preference is a function of the particular kind of education found in that school; Nigerian children in Koranic schools memorize the Koran in Arabic without being able to understand a word of that language. The teachers in many African schools are themselves poorly educated by Western standards, and Serpell speculates that they do not put as much emphasis as their European counterparts on the kind of learning that leads to the development of form preferences.

Before we jump to sweeping conclusions about the significance of various stimulus preferences in these selection experiments, we should ask ourselves how general and consistent the observed preferences are and the extent to which they depend on the particular measure used. All too often very broad generalizations are made on the basis of a single study using a single method of experimentation.

As an example of some of the problems involved, we shall present data gathered by our own research group in Liberia. The first experiment* used a technique very similar to that employed by Suchman and Trabasso (1966), in which stimuli could be matched on the basis of color or form. There was only a slight preference for color over form among illiterate children aged 6 to 8 and 10 to 14 years (53 percent), with the preference changing to form for matched age mates attending local schools (66 percent). However, if the stimuli permitted three ways of matching—on color, form, or size (large red triangle, large white square, and small white triangle)—there was a preference for *form* instead of color for the illiterate children (77 percent) and an increased preference for form among the schoolchildren (also 77 percent). Ciborowski's results suggest that the preference for one dimension over another is *not* absolute. It depends upon the context of the stimulus choices experienced by the subject.

A second experiment, by Sharp, measured preferences of Liberian children for color, form, and number, using a slightly different technique. Subjects were shown pairs of cards, each of which contained figures that differed in three dimensions. For instance, one card might contain three red triangles, the other two black squares. The subject was asked to choose one of the cards and to describe the picture on it so that the experimenter could pick it out. Subjects' responses were scored according to which attributes were mentioned and whether they mentioned one, two, or three of the attributes of the card they had in mind ("it's the red one"; "it's the one with the two red triangles").

On the basis of this measure of preference (which aspect of the stimuli a subject chooses to talk about when communicating to someone else), these subjects (who were of different ages and different educational levels) would be classed as having a strong bias toward color, with number second, and form weakest. But these subjects are from the same population as that studied by Ciborowski with very similar material (except that his included size as a third dimension while Sharp's included number).

We have to conclude that stimulus preferences are *not* a fixed

---

*This experiment was conducted by T. Ciborowski (in Cole, Gay, Glick, and Sharp, 1971).

property of the individual studied. They are very sensitive to a number of variables, including age, education, the particular stimulus dimensions present when the choice is made, and the method used to test for preference.

In view of all these complexities, one might well ask whether any significance can be attached to subjects' preferences for one stimulus attribute over another. Certain aspects of this research do seem to be significant. There is the repeated occurrence of a stable preference for color in young European and American children, which is converted into a preference for form at the age of 4 to 5. Evidence from other cultures indicates that form preference does not always occur, or does not occur in so marked a fashion. When color is dominant, it may remain so. Or, in some cases, a color–form shift occurs if children attend European-style schools. This suggests that the developmental trend observed in European and American children is connected in some way with the experiences that result from formal schooling. Many investigators hypothesize that sensitivity to printed words is an important factor in promoting a form preference, although this idea remains a speculation at the present time.

Summary

Referring back to the questions we posed at the beginning of this chapter (p. 64), we can see that many culturally linked variations in perceptual behavior have been demonstrated by cross-cultural research. Once we go beyond this simple generalization, however, a multitude of difficulties sets in. Once again we get enmeshed in the question of what kinds of behavior we want to call "perceptual" and in problems of determining what, exactly, is controlling the behavior we observe.

To begin with, we can be fairly confident that our modes of responding to pictures and diagrams (two-dimensional representations of three-dimensional scenes and objects) are not experience free; they depend in some way upon our past histories of dealing with such materials. Note that we use the term "responding to pictures," not "perceiving pictures." This distinction seems necessary in that the studies demonstrate that our inferences about what a person "saw" depend on what kind of response we ask him to make; describing a pictorial representation and making a model of it are different tasks and yield different interpretations of underlying perceptual processes. In a way, this may be seen as a parallel problem to that of drawing what we see. When African children draw a profile of a cow with four legs and two eyes, we do not attribute this to x-ray vision, but to habits of representation. The studies reviewed here leave us wondering whether the same cannot be said of two-dimensional responders.

A closely related problem has to do with the conditions that promote two-dimensional responses. Several reports seem to indicate that African children continue to respond two-dimensionally even after years of European-style schooling, while others claim differences after just a little exposure. This issue has not been resolved.

A recent theory of perceptual development put forward by Olson (1970) may offer the possibility of resolving some of the inconsistent findings with respect to perception of pictorial material. In a series of studies of children's perception of diagonality, he found that what the child "saw" in a geometric pattern presented by the experimenter was related to what action he was asked to perform —whether he was to recognize the pattern, to copy it, or to reconstruct it. Olson maintains that various forms of activity require different perceptual information, and that the child elaborates his perceptual world (makes new and different discriminations) as he masters new activities. For example, creeping around a room or walking across a field requires information based primarily on topological cues, whereas building a wooden crate requires information based on geometric features. "You require different cues to catch a ball than to discriminate it from a cup" (Olson, 1970, p. 201). Different activities—such as locomotion, speaking a language, writing a language, drawing, carving—proceed in different media. When a person attempts to perform in a new medium— say, he is learning to draw—he has to attend to and select new cues or information from the perceptual world in order to meet the demands of this specific medium: "Performatory attempts in representational art, geometric drawing, and constructing require, for their guidance, perceptual information that is somewhat unique to that medium. To state this point in the form of an aphorism: 'squares did not have equal sides and equal angles until one attempted to draw them.' " (Olson, 1970, p. 202).

This approach seems to tie in very well with Dawson's training program in pictorial depth perception. He asked young men to draw scenes requiring representation of depth cues, and he gave them experience in comparing their drawings with the original scene. In Olson's terms, the activity of drawing required selection and attention to particular cues containing distance information in the real-world scene, cues that otherwise may have gone unnoticed.

Olson's position clearly has important implications for cross-cultural research on many issues of perception, in addition to those involved in the restricted domain of picture perception. One of its especially interesting features is that it draws the attention of psychologists to the range of media and technical activities provided by different cultures as a possible source of cognitive differences among the people of different cultures.

This same comment applies to the work on selectivity in perception, an area that has generated a good deal of work, but about which much remains uncertain.

Some of the questions that concern us most are the following:

1. Almost all of the research on selectivity in perception (except for that using the binocular rivalry technique) employs abstract stimuli and makes a "correct answer" dependent on some special attribute (such as color). There have been no studies of responses to embedded figures using locally significant stimulus objects, and only a few studies of attribute preferences have used meaningful objects.

2. Although it has rarely been systematically investigated, we can be fairly confident that the kind of response a subject is asked to make (drawing, speaking, matching figures by pointing) affects the kinds of perceptual processes that we conclude he has. Some hint of this comes from our own work in Liberia, where asking people to sort cards and asking them to describe them seem to lead to different conclusions about stimulus preference. But what about studies involving embedded figures? Might it not also be the case that the way a subject is asked to respond affects what he "sees" in the embedded figure? We think it possible (and in accord with Olson's 1970 findings), but know of no data on the problem.

3. Finally, we are concerned that all but one of the studies reported (that by Wober) rely exclusively on the visual mode to make inferences that are often not mode-dependent. Certainly those who are engaged in work on field-dependence do not think that they are studying the visual field alone. Yet in relying on visual material they are courting difficulties, some of which we have discussed above. When this question of stimulus modality and the question of response requirements are combined, we can see the possibility of some serious problems. For ex-

ample, Wober found less field-dependence in Africans on a test in which somatosensory information (proprioceptive cues) was available (rod-and-frame test) than on a test presenting visual information only (embedded figures test). But in switching tests, he not only added information in a new sensory modality, he changed the response requirements of the task as well. Instead of being required to outline or name a figure, his subjects had to adjust a rod—a three-dimensional object in the real world. Which component determined the results he reports?

Finally, it is worth emphasizing that all of the research on culture and perception discussed in this chapter leaves open the question of cultural differences in the perception of naturally occurring visual scenes. We know that there is something special about perceiving depth cues in pictures, but is there any evidence of cultural differences in depth perception when the person being studied is observing a natural scene? We know of no systematic data on this point, but anecdotal evidence indicates that there may indeed be cultural (or at least, experiential) influences on perception for natural scenes. For example, Turnbull (1961) in his ethnography of the pygmies of the Iturbi forest relates an incident in which a pygmy accompanies him out of the forest. At one point there is an opportunity to see some cows, grazing in the distance. The pygmy, who knows what cows are, but who has never had the opportunity to see one at a great distance, thinks that he is looking at ants! We have observed a similar phenomenon when a jungle-raised Kpelle child is taken at around age 10 to the capital city of Monrovia, where large tanker ships can be seen far at sea from a tall hotel on a hilltop. The child, who had never seen such a view before and was not familiar with tankers, commented on the bravery of men who would go out to sea in such small boats. These anecdotes suggest, among other things, that it would be interesting and theoretically profitable, to arrange some "natural" perceptual experiments to test out the generality of laboratory-generated phenomena.

It should be clear to the reader, as it is to us, that a great deal of research remains to be done before the kinds of questions about culture and perception that we have asked, as well as questions we have not been astute enough to think of, are answered.

chapter 5 *Culture and Conceptual Processes*

Discussions of cultural variations in thought processes often emphasize that a major source of group differences is in the "ways of classifying the world" that characterize a given cultural group. "Ways of classifying" is also a useful bridge between the experiments on perceptual processes discussed in the previous chapter, and experiments on conceptual processes, which we will discuss in this chapter.

When we closely examine statements by psychologists about perception and conception, it becomes apparent that the data we previously discussed as a matter of perceptual preference may be viewed just as easily in terms of elementary conceptual groupings or classifications. All of these are pyschological processes* by which we treat as "similar" or "equivalent" phenomena that

---

*For present purposes, we will not make any distinctions among the terms *classification, concept* or *category*, although it should be understood by the reader that there are many different psychological concepts of a *concept*.

vary in some way among themselves. No two roses are identical, but they are commonly experienced as interchangable members of the class of roses; a rose and a dandelion are physically even more unlike, but are "similar" members of a class of flowers; and together with an oak tree, a frog, and an infant, roses and dandelions are "alike" with respect to their inclusion in a class of living things. As these examples illustrate, there is a whole multiplicity of processes by which we deal with environmental variability, reducing or holding differences constant and establishing similarity or equivalence as a basis for action and thought. These processes may vary with the attributes of the things in question, the context in which the act of classifying occurs, and the skills and knowledge we possess.

When similarity among things is defined in terms of their physical attributes, the act of classifying may be considered close to perception. For example, when considering neighboring points on the color spectrum, it seems at least possible that true lack of discrimination in some sensory sense is occurring when subjects respond with a single term to two different colors. When a person says "red" to a set of color chips that we know to be discriminably different, it may still be possible to give a perceptual interpretation by arguing that the subject perceives all of the hues to be the same. But why speak of a perceptual process when one is dealing with a set of stimuli consisting of a black triangle, a red triangle, and a red square? Surely the subject can discriminate among these objects. A more appropriate method of characterizing the subject's choices when he says that two of the objects are the same is to consider them ways of classifying objects in the environment.

Bases for Classification

In studies of classification, both in developmental and cross-cultural psychology, a good deal of interest has centered on two aspects of the subject's performance: (1) the particular attribute the subject uses as the criterion of similarity (this is comparable to interest in the stimulus dimension in perceptual preference studies), and (2) whether or not he uses a single attribute consistently as the basis for grouping. Findings with respect to these questions have provided much of the empirical foundation for theories of cognitive development that stress progression from a kind of thinking that is concrete and context-bound to thinking that is abstract and rule-governed. Results from cross-cultural studies of classification have led several authors to characterize the thinking of nonindustrialized people as concrete and deficient in the abstract attitude. In Chapter 2, we showed how scholars with such contrasting points of view as Claude Levi-Strauss, the structural anthropologist, and Heinz Werner, the developmental psychologist, share a common interest in analyzing the concepts and classifications employed in primitive cultures.

As the examples at the beginning of this chapter indicate, the notion of *class* or *concept* is used very broadly by psychologists to refer to a wide range of grouping operations. Theories that have been developed to explain classificatory behavior have usually been tied in closely to the particular set of operations an investigator has chosen to study. Jerome Bruner's theory of cognitive growth furnishes a useful framework for examining current research in this area. It has generated specific hypotheses about effects of cultural institutions on classification, and these hypotheses have been explored in cross-cultural settings. Conceptual development, according to Bruner, involves a shift in what features of the world the child uses as a basis for defining how things are alike (what we have called the criterial attribute). Very young American children tend to treat items as equivalent on the basis of *perceptual* qualities, such as color, size, shape, or position. With intellectual growth, the child breaks away from this perceptual dominance and bases his classifications on *functional* attributes—what things can do or what a person can do with things. He also increasingly comes to group items together under a common *class name*.

Bruner asserts further that along with the change in favored attribute, there is an orderly progression in the *operations* by which the child combines things. Initially, the child will form loose groupings or "collections"—in which he uses a variety of characteristics and associations among the items. Gradually the child works his way toward "true conceptual groupings based on the rule of the superordinate class"—that is, toward groupings based on some *single common* feature that characterizes all the items included within the group and none of the items excluded from it. To put it still another way, the child operates with a single rule governing admission of an item into the group.

While Bruner does not use the terms *concrete* or *abstract* in his discussion of these different aspects of grouping performance, these terms have classically been used to differentiate the young child's performance from that of the older child. A classification based on a perceptual characteristic is usually considered to be concrete. For some theorists, only a nonperceptual grouping based on a class name or nonphysical property (such as animate, edible, mammal) qualifies as "abstract." The term *abstract* has also been used to refer to the operation by which one common characteristic is singled out (i.e., abstracted) and used to unite the items being worked with. From this point of view, Bruner's superordinate, single-rule grouping indicates a more abstract level of thought than groupings making use of multiple criteria.

With these distinctions in mind, we will turn to consideration of an extensive investigation of the cultural influence on classifying conducted by Patricia Greenfield, a colleague of Bruner's (Bruner, Olver, and Greenfield, 1966). Data were gathered from children of the Wolof tribe in rural Senegal, using a sorting procedure similar to the preference studies described in the previous chapter, but with some important differences. Ten familiar objects were laid on a table in front of the child, who was asked to "pick those that belong together." The set contained four articles of clothing, four round objects, and four red objects (one of which was an article of clothing and one a round object), permitting the child to form groups according to function, form, or color.

If the items that were selected conformed to one of these classes (color, form, or function), the child was credited with applying a consistent classification rule. Figure 5–1 plots the percentage of nonschooled tribal children at each age level who consistently applied any of the possible classification rules. It can be seen from the graph that by the age of 15, virtually every Wolof child is making a systematic classification of the objects. A majority of these children based their classifications on color, and the authors conclude that "the change in grouping structure with age consists primarily, then, in learning to apply the color rule systematically" (p. 286). In terms of *preference*, these results fit in nicely with the findings on color dominance reviewed in the previous section, but the interpretation here is *con*ceptual, not *per*ceptual.

A further study by Greenfield among the Wolof used sets of

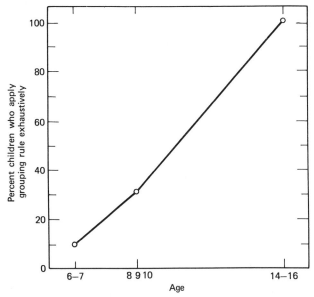

Figure 5-1. Percentage of unschooled Wolof village children who apply grouping rule exhaustively.

pictures mounted on cards. The cards were designed so that within each set it was possible to form pairs based on the color, form, or function of the object pictured on the card (see Figure 5–2). The child was first asked to show the experimenter which of the two pictures in a set were "most alike." He was then asked, "Why are they most alike?" Subjects were selected from three populations: (1) traditional people from the bush who had not attended school —ages 6 to 7, 8 to 9, 11 to 13, and adults; (2) schoolchildren from the same town, and (3) schoolchildren living in Dakar, the capital city of Senegal.

This experiment produced many interesting results. Among the most important for understanding the issue discussed here is that schooling apparently exerted a very strong influence on the way classifications were made and on the kinds of reasons subjects gave for the classes they formed. Children who had attended school, whether from the small bush village or the city, performed very much as American children did; preference for color decreased sharply with grade, while form and function preferences increased. Furthermore, an increasing proportion of the older children justified their classification in terms of a superordinate cate-

Set 1

Color: yellow

Shape: round

Function: to eat

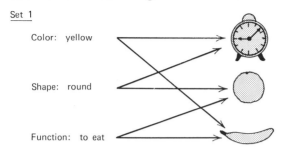

Set 2

Color: orange

Shape:

Function: to wear

Set 3

Color: blue

Shape:

Function: to ride

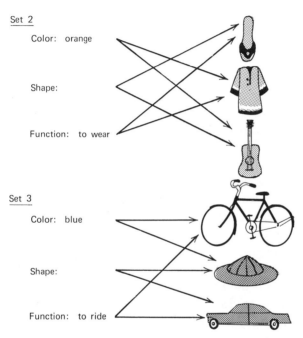

Figure 5-2. Three picture displays in Wolof classification study, with their attributes. *Set 1*, clock, orange, and banana; *Set 2*, sandal, *bubu* (Wolof robe), and guitar; *Set 3*, bicycle, helmet, and car.

gory ("it's the round ones"). The children who had not attended school and lived in the bush responded quite differently. Such children showed *greater* preference for color with increasing age and rarely justified their responses by noting the category to which the pictures belonged. The authors make the following comments about how the course of development of schoolchildren differed from that of children who were not in school:

This perceptual development is basically a conceptual one. . . . By conceptual we mean that school is teaching European habits of perceptual *analysis*. An analysis into parts is plainly crucial to concepts based on the multi-dimensional attributes of form, whereas unitary global perception could suffice for color grouping (Bruner, Olver, and Greenfield, 1966, p. 316).

Bruner and his colleagues feel that their results are also pertinent to observations made by various anthropologists and psychologists to the effect that the early cognitive development of primitive peoples is quite rapid, but that primitive children's development stops much earlier than that of European children. European children develop more slowly at first, but their development continues through adolescence. In the experiment just presented, the evidence for this idea is that nonschooled children fail to develop a form preference and fail to provide categorial justifications for their choices. Taken together with the fact that children who attend school do show the shift from color to form preference, these findings suggested to Greenfield and Bruner that leveling off of cognitive development occurs because children lack the experiences provided by the school. In this view, African children who have attended school are "European" in their development. Although no one can be sure how schooling exerts its effect, Bruner and his colleagues speculate that the school makes complex demands on the growing child, forcing him to develop new intellectual tools in order to keep up. One of these tools is the kind of perceptual analysis that underlies form classification.

Many questions are raised by this interpretation. One that immediately comes to mind is what significance should be attached to the subject's selection of a particular attribute when he is given only one opportunity to make a choice. If a child chooses color, does this mean that he does not have the capacity to group by form or only that he *prefers* to group by color? We might also ask a prior question. When a set of stimuli allows for several bases of classification, the choice of a classification rule is often arbitrary (color, form, and function are all logically consistent classification schemes). Do people realize this fact? When a person groups a set of cards or objects on, say, the basis of color, is he expressing a preference among a set of alternatives, or is he performing what he considers to be *the* (one and only) correct classification? In short, does he recognize that there are other possible ways of classifying the items? (An analogy here would be the ways in which members of a family could be grouped: as males and females, as parents and children, or as members of the nuclear family and members of the extended family).

Classification and Reclassification

Sharp and Cole (in an unpublished experiment) attempted to get at these questions. Working in Yucatan, Mexico, where the educational experience of Mayan people is quite variable, they presented to people of various ages and educational backgrounds the set of cards depicted in Figure 5–3. The cards were laid out in a haphazard arrangement on a small table in front of the subject, and he was asked to place them into piles so that the cards in each pile were alike in some way. He was not told what was meant by the term *alike*. No restriction was placed on the number of piles a subject could make, but the stimuli were clearly divisible along the dimensions of color, form, and number. On all but a few occasions, subjects placed the cards in two piles. But it was by no means the case that the two piles were chosen in a manner consistent with one of the three preselected dimensions.

For subjects who did sort the cards into two piles in terms of color, form, or number, the cards were then shuffled and the person was asked to find a different way to form piles that were alike.

The subjects in this experiment were children and young adults living in rural towns. The youngest children were 6 to 8 years old and were enrolled in the first grade. In addition, there was a group of 9- to 10-year-olds (in the third grade), a group of 12- to 13-year-olds (sixth grade), and a group of teenagers (15 to 20 years old) who had attended no more than three years of school.

To begin with, it was found that not everyone was successful in arriving at a partition of the cards according to one of the three specified stimulus dimensions (using a single rule). The percentage of successful initial classifications for the first-, third-, and sixth-graders was 17, 47, and 84 percent, respectively. These data indicate a reliable increase in the likelihood of a dimensional classification as school children grow older. But the results from the teenagers indicated that sorting of these materials was con-

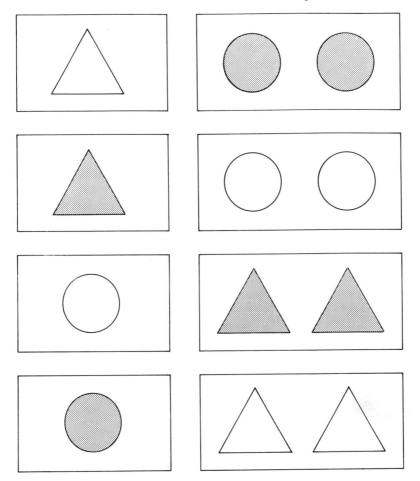

Figure 5-3. Cards used in Mexican reclassification study. Objects portrayed vary in color (black and red), form (circle and triangle), and number (one and two).

ditioned much more by educational experience than by age alone. The teenagers averaged 37 percent correct sorts. This is between the levels for the first- and third-graders, and is consistent with the average educational level of 1.4 years for the teenagers. The relation between education and classification is even more striking when the performance of the teenagers is calculated separately for those who had never attended school or had attended only one year and for those who had attended two or three years. For the relatively uneducated group of teenagers, there were 25 percent correct sorts, while the more educated teenagers sorted correctly 52 percent of the time.

When subjects were asked to classify the cards in a new way, very little reclassification was observed among the first-graders. Only one of the 32 children in this age group successfully re-sorted the cards consistent with a new dimension. Third-graders (44 percent) were more successful in finding a new, consistent sorting scheme, and a majority of the sixth-graders (60 percent) were successful. Again the performance of more poorly educated among the teenagers implicates education in the development of skilled performance in this classification task. Only two teenagers with one year of education or less (8 percent of those tested) reclassified the cards. Those teenagers with two or three years of education responded similarly to the third-graders (28 percent correct re-sorts).

These results from rural Yucatan support and extend the analysis offered by Greenfield and Bruner on the basis of their studies in Senegal. Two points stand out. First, success in classifying arbitrary sets of multi-attribute stimuli like those used in these studies is much more influenced by years of education than chronological age *per se*. This result should make us very cautious about the interpretation of developmental changes in similar classification behaviors observed in the United States or Europe, where age and educational experience co-vary almost perfectly. Secondly, we can see that classification and reclassification are not necessarily the result of the same process—many subjects who could make a single classification could not reclassify the set of cards along another dimension. It seems quite possible that one consequence of educational experience is to instill the notion that any set of objects can be treated (classified) in a varity of ways— there is no "one correct way," regardless of the task at hand. There has been relatively little work done on the problem of reclassification, either intra-culturally or cross-culturally (see, however, Goldstein and Scheerer, 1941).

Generalizing Rules of Classification

The study just described illustrates the problems that arise when uneducated people are asked to change the classification rule that they have been using in sorting a set of material. The study to be described in this section turns the question around and asks what problems may be involved in carrying over the *same* classification rule from one problem to another. If someone is taught a particular classification rule, will he apply this rule to other problems of the same kind? Does the fact that someone learns to make "correct" classifications imply that he has learned a general rule applying to classification?

To answer some of these questions, Sharp (1971) conducted a study in which he taught Kpelle children to classify material according to attributes the experimenter defined as correct.

Sharp's stimuli were figures on cards which differed in form (triangle, circle, square), color (red, blue, black), number (two, three, four). Subjects were not presented the cards all at once but were shown pairs of cards differing along all three dimensions (for example, two red triangles on one and four black circles on the other). The subject's task was to say which of the cards the experimenter was thinking of, and he was informed after each decision whether or not he was correct. For example, the correct cards for the first problem might be the blue ones, regardless of the forms depicted or the number of figures on the card. Subjects continued responding until they were correct 9 trials in a row or until 40 trials had been presented. Then they were given a second and a third problem, in which the task remained the same but the attribute that defined the correct cards changed for each problem.

Sharp was interested in learning whether children would show improvement on this task as a result of practice: Would they solve the second and third problems faster than the first if the dimension of solution (color in our example) remained unchanged?

Two kinds of practice were studied. (a) Three problems were presented, all involving the dimension of color, but a different color was correct on each. (b) Three problems were presented on which the correct dimension was different each time (color on the first, form on the second, number on the third, for example).

These two kinds of repeated practice allowed Sharp to distinguish between two kinds of improvement—generalized transfer resulting from practice in learning this type of problem, and specific transfer resulting from learning about particular dimensions.

Sharp's children were selected from three groups: a group of 6- to 8-year-olds who did not attend school, a group of 12- to 14-

year-olds who did not attend school, and 12- to 14-year-olds in the fourth to sixth grades. This selection allowed comparisons of performance as a function of age and education.

Figure 5–4 shows the results for each of the groups given three problems in which the same dimension remained correct. The figure is divided into three graphs, one for each group. The data points in each graph represent the average number of trials needed to learn a given problem. For example, the 6- to 8-year-old non-educated children learned their first color problem in an average of 8.5 trials, their second in 7.2 trials, and their third in 6.9. The other graphs are to be interpreted in the same way.

The influence of stimulus preference is very clearly evident: for all three groups, color is learned in fewer trials than number, and form is most difficult of all. Moreover, older children learn more rapidly than younger ones, and the educated children learn more rapidly than the noneducated children.

The second important feature of these data is that the older children seem to *improve* from one problem to the next, but for the 6- to 8-year-olds there is little improvement from problem to problem.

The source of problem-to-problem improvement was investigated by looking at the performance of the children for whom the correct dimension was changed from one problem to the next. (These data are not shown.) If the problem-to-problem improvement was the result of some general factor (such as increased familiarity with the task), we should expect improvement even when the particular dimension changed. However, no problem-to-problem improvement was observed; it took just as long to learn the third problem as it did to learn the first.

Taken together, these results strongly suggest that for the amount of practice given (three problems is by no means a lot of practice), improvement from one problem to the next (often termed *learning to learn*) occurs only if subjects learn to attend to a particular dimension. There is no generalized learning to learn. It appears that the older subjects must be doing something like saying to themselves, "if red was correct last time, one of the colors must be correct this time." This strategy works only if the correct dimension remains the same from problem to problem.

This plausible analysis leaves an unanswered question: How do the younger, noneducated children learn these problems if they do not select out a particular dimension and then learn what

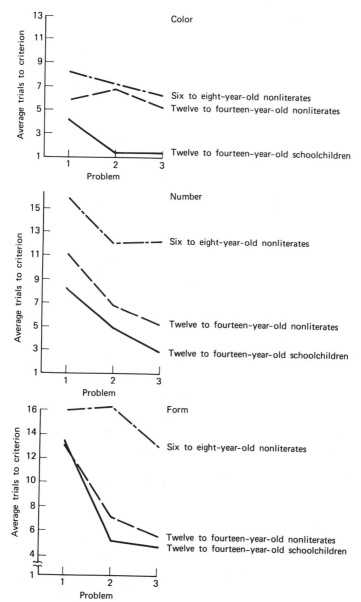

Figure 5-4. Problem-to-problem improvement in classification among Kpelle children. Each panel of the figure shows learning scores for children trained to classify on a different dimension (color, number, or form).

the correct value on that dimension is? These children learn more slowly than their educated brethren, but *how* do they learn?

A major alternative to learning about dimensions was to learn which particular cards were called "correct."

Instead of learning "it's the red ones," the younger children may have been learning to choose four specific cards (one red circle, one red square, two red circles, two red squares). If so, there would be no basis for improvement in performance from one problem to the next, since the particular cards were changed for each problem.

To determine whether this was actually the case, we need to examine the trial-by-trial learning rate. We can begin by asking ourselves: What kind of data would be produced if subjects learned to solve these classification problems by searching for the correct attribute ("two" or "black," for example)? Since the correct attribute is present on exactly half the cards, the subject ought to have a 50–50 chance of identifying it on any trial. Once he has identified it, he ought to be correct 100 percent of the time.

However, what if the subject learned by remembering specific "correct cards"? At first he, too, would be guessing with a 50–50 chance of being right. But when a card reappeared, he would not have to guess if he remembered it. He would only guess at the unlearned cards. Thus, his performance on the set of cards, taken as a whole, would improve gradually from trial to trial until all the cards were learned.

With this in mind, let us examine the performances of the younger and older Kpelle children, looking for evidence of two patterns of performance *prior* to *solution* of the problem. We expect to find the performance of the older children at a chance level prior to solution, at which point correct answers will jump to 100 percent; but the performance of the younger children should show gradual improvement, beginning at 50 percent and slowly approaching 100 percent.*

This is exactly the pattern of performance obtained. Figure 5–5 shows examples of the *pre-solution* performances of noneducated 6- to 8-year-olds and groups of educated and noneducated 12- to 14-year-olds solving a form problem. Consistent with our analysis, performance of the 6- to 8-year-old children improves gradually

*See Cole et al., 1971, chap. 5, for a full account of the techniques of data analysis used in this evaluation.

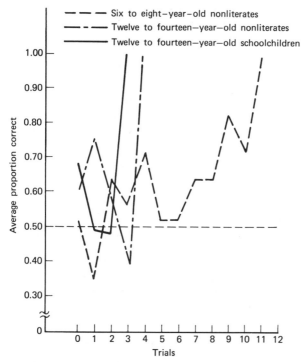

Figure 5-5. Presolution performance of children learning to classify on the basis of form.

prior to solution, while the two groups of older children respond at random until the point of solution.

We find these data interesting for a variety of reasons. In the first place, they illustrate the need to consider stimulus *preferences* when making comparative judgments about issues like the rate of learning. They isolate the basis of improvement in learning to classify, in those cases where improvement occurs. And, third, they suggest that the source of the difference between older and younger children is the tendency of the latter to learn these problems as a set of specific instances, while the older children learn by selecting out the relevant attribute.

These results bear on the larger issue of cultural differences in learning, because, among other reasons, the performance of the younger children is a classic case of rote learning (i.e., memorizing specific instances) in a problem the older children treat conceptually.

But is this rote learning, which is so often castigated in discussions of education and so often attributed to African children, a poor way to learn this problem (poor in the sense of inefficient)? Is it the only way these children *can* learn a classification problem? Almost certainly not.

To begin with, learning by rote is an efficient way to learn if there are only a few instances. In such cases, searching for the correct attribute may require more trials than committing four instances to memory.

There are also studies of classification learning among these same groups of uneducated people that give clear evidence of conceptual learning. For example, Gay and Cole (1967) presented children problems similar to Sharp's except that there were many examples, so that a particular example was rarely, if ever, repeated. Since the examples were not repeated, the children obviously could not be responding correctly on the basis of rote learning of specific instances. We therefore must conclude that young uneducated Kpelle children *can* learn pictorial classification problems *conceptually*.

This brings us back to a reoccurring theme: how a thing is learned or perceived depends not only on the past experience of the subject (which is certainly a factor), but also on the demands of the task presented him. In this case we can expect simple rote learning by certain subjects in some circumstances, but not in others. American school children tend to abandon the rote strategy even for simple problems, while the young Liberian non-schooled child maintains it unless the conditions of the problem make it too difficult.

Influence of Content on Classification

One problem that arises in connection with all of the studies described is to determine how specialized the results are. Can we safely generalize from experiments with pictures on cards to the larger domain of real-life classification? To raise only a few questions: We know that nonschooled traditional Africans have difficulty in the perception of two-dimensional pictures. Does this difficulty affect the attributes that they choose for classification? Would the same classifications occur if we *said* the names of the objects instead of showing pictures of them? How does the way in which the pictures are classified relate to natural-language categories? For example, we suspect that an anlysis of the Wolof language would almost certainly reveal that cow, tree trunk, and mud are *not* classified together, although these things might well be classified together under the color category brown, if shown on picture cards. Almost certainly cow is part of a semantic category containing goat, sheep, and pig whereas tree, bush, vine, and grass might be part of another class. Exactly the same remarks apply to the Mayans in Yucatan or to any other cultural group.

Several investigations in recent years have been concerned with exactly these kinds of problems. Dominant in this research has been the question: To what extent is the classifying behavior specific to the materials being classified?

Some investigators have been very concerned with the *kind of materials* to be sorted. In Greenfield's work it did not seem to make much difference whether children were presented objects or pictures; nonschooled children still chose color. But this has not usually been the case.

For example, Deregowski and Serpell (1971) conducted a study using photographs and real objects in a comparison of the classifications of Zambian and Scottish school children and found that the pictures and objects were *not* identically classified. Their subjects were third grade students from the Scottish city of Aberdeen and the Zambian city of Lusaka.

Each subject population was divided into three groups. The first group was asked to name and classify eight toy objects consisting of four vehicles and four animals. Within each of these two main subclasses, the objects could be grouped into pairs. For the vehicles the subgroupings could be in terms of color or function (do they carry people or cargo). For the animals the pairing could be based on color or domesticity (domestic or wild). The second group of subjects was asked to name and classify color photographs of these toys, and the third group was asked to name and classify black-and-white photographs.

Since the two major classifications could be broken down into pair subclasses, Deregowski and Serpell asked each subject who produced groupings of three or more stimuli to further subdivide them. They also asked for the reason underlying the subject's final classification.

When the task was sorting pictures, the Scottish children

showed a marked superiority. They spontaneously formed four subclasses without prompting, while many of the Zambian children produced subclasses only after they had explicitly been asked to break down their larger classes. However, when the task was sorting models, there were no differences in this regard between the children from the two populations—both groups spontaneously sorted the objects into two main groups with two subgroups in each. These results emphasize the fact that pictures and the objects they depict cannot be considered equivalent stimuli for the Zambian children, although they are roughly equivalent for the Scottish children.

Other differences between the two populations were observed, in addition to the number of subclasses the children produced. For one thing, the subgroups produced by the Zambian children were much more likely to be based on color than were the Scottish children's subgroups. The Zambian children were also less likely to give an adequate verbal explanation for the principle underlying the sorting they arrived at. For example, only 29 percent of the Zambian children adequately explained their separation of vehicles into passenger and cargo vehicles, while 95 percent of the Scottish children did so.

Deregowski and Serpell's research points out the relevance of the physical representation of the material (photograph or object) used in the classification task. A closely related problem is one of *familiarity*. The best-known study of this problem was conducted by Price-Williams (1962) among educated and noneducated children in Nigeria.

Price-Williams was unhappy with the fact that many studies of classification among African children employed stimuli such as those in Figure 5–3—triangles, squares, and other idealized forms that were unfamiliar and of no revelance to the children being tested. So he decided to carry out his work on classification using two familiar and easily identified domains—animals and plants that every Tiv child was familiar with. For this purpose, he picked ten different kinds of animals, varying in such aspects as color, size, edibility, etc. He also picked ten different kinds of plants that could be classified in terms of size, edibility, location (near river or on top of hill), and other principles.

He asked the children to carry out two tasks with each of these sets of objects (he used small plastic dolls for most of the animals,

except for a beetle and a fish). First, the child was asked to
select those objects that belonged together and to tell why he
did so. After each selection and grouping, the child was asked
whether he could discover another way of grouping the objects.
This procedure was continued until the child declared that there
were no other ways to group the objects.

Price-Williams's approach produced two outstanding results.
Even the youngest children studied (6 years old) could and did
classify the objects. Furthermore, all the children reclassified the
objects when asked to do so; the youngest children found three
to four ways of grouping, while the 11-year-olds found about six.
Price-Williams did *not* find any consistent difference between educated and noneducated children using these objects as stimuli.

One other result obtained by Price-Williams is of particular
interest. When he scored the children's justifications for their
groupings, he found that when *animals* were grouped, the children
tended to justify the groups they made in terms of concrete attributes like their color, size, or the place where they are found.
When grouping *plants*, these same children overwhelmingly justified their response in terms of the abstract feature of edibility.
This result makes the very important point that we cannot speak
of abstract and concrete thinking in general. Not only the familiarity and form of physical respresentation of the things classified,
but the specific domains from which the items are drawn, appear
to influence the abstractness of the responses given.

A similar message concerning the importance of the domain
of objects being classified is illustrated in a recent study by Irwin
and McLaughlin (1970). They used stimulus cards with pictures
of triangles and squares much like those employed by Sharp and
Cole (see Figure 5–3); in addition, they made up a task that was
identical in *principle*, but different in material content. Some
subjects in the study were asked to classify and reclassify eight
bowls of rice: the bowls were large or small, the rice was polished
or rough, and two kinds of rice were used. Working with Mano
rice farmers and schoolchildren in central Liberia, Irwin and
McLauglin wanted to see whether the farmers could find alternative ways of classifying the bowls of rice more easily than they
could find alternative classification for the cards with triangles
and squares. Consistent with the results of Sharp and Cole, Mano
nonliterate adults were not as good as the schoolchildren at

finding more than a single basis for classifying the cards. But they were about as good at classifying the rice bowls as the school–children were at classifying the cards! In this study the *content* of the material was not varied independently of the *form* of the material (rice bowls are *real* objects as contrasted with pictorial representations of triangles). Nevertheless, it is a very clear example of how our inferences about the effect of schooling are modified by our knowledge that with some materials, nonschooled people produce classifications that we might otherwise have concluded to be beyond their capacities.

Separating Education from Other Cultural Variations

Our inferences about the effects of schooling might also be modified if we took into account other life experiences that might modify the way traditional people approached a task of classification.

One difficulty with most of the research on culture and classification discussed so far is that comparisons almost always take the form of pitting "civilized" (educated) and "primitive" societies against each other; yet there are clearly wide variations in degree of exposure to modern influences even among nonliterate peoples. Scribner (in unpublished research) secured extensive data on sorting behavior of Kpelle tribal children and adults who had varying degrees of involvement in Western-style living as well as education. The materials to be sorted consisted of 25 very familiar and common objects belonging to categories of hunting implements, foods, cooking utensils, clothes, and sewing things.

Previous research had shown that these categories are part of a hierarchically organized system used by the Kpelle to divide things into subdivisions: utensils and food, for example, are categories or classes under a more general head of *household things*, which is part of a larger class of *working things*. We refer to these as *taxonomic* categories and sometimes, because of the use of the term in this line of psychological research, as *semantic* categories. When individuals group items on the basis of their taxonomic class membership, this is taken by some psychologists to be evidence of abstract thinking.

The particular categories used in this study were selected because they provided items that could be linked together by an action sequence across classes just as easily as by membership in a common class. (The needle, scissors, and shirt can be put together, for example, because you can use sewing items to make an article of clothing). As was true for one of the Greenfield studies described earlier, this dual possibility permitted Scribner to assess the relative probabilities of the two ways of sorting, instead of restricting subjects to the one "correct" way.

Subjects were asked to sort the objects into groups of things that "go together." They were constrained to have no less than three items in a group. Once a classification of the objects was obtained, they were given additional sorting trials until they achieved exactly the same grouping of all the items on two successive trials. This procedure made it possible to examine the *stable* bases used for grouping rather than those "first used."

Adult subject populations were high school students, nonliterate adults from a transitional-type village holding cash jobs (cash workers), nonliterate rice farmers from a traditional village on a road (road village), and nonliterate rice farmers from a traditional bush village five hours from the nearest road (bush village). In addition, there were matched groups of schoolchildren and nonschool children in the 10- to 14-year-old age group (fourth through sixth grades) and in the 6- to 8-year-old age group (first grade).

The groupings produced by subjects were scored on the basis of how many members of a given taxonomic category (food, clothes, etc.) appeared together in the subject's final groupings.

High-schoolers, as expected, almost uniformly grouped items by taxonomic category; cash workers and road villagers also predominantly made category groupings, although none of these men and women had any formal schooling and none could read or write. The use of category membership as a grouping principle dropped off sharply with the bush villagers, but analysis of the items they put together still showed some category influence. Now consider the child subjects. The young ones (6- to 8-year-olds) virtually ignored the categories when grouping, whether or not they were in school; their groups were frequently idiosyncratic, as the following examples illustrate: gun, peanut, and belt; net, headtie, knife, cap, and peanut; needle, potato, and shirt.

The 10- to 14-year-old nonschooled children were not much different from the 6- to 8-year olds, but their schooled counterparts made groups corresponding to some extent to the semantic categories. Here we would seem to have another piece of evidence of the effect of schooling on classifying behavior; we might be inclined, as was Greenfield, to attribute the observed change solely to education, except for one fact: adult village groups, none of whom had had any schooling whatsoever, performed on a par with, or above, the 10- to 14-year-old schoolchildren! This result not only suggests caution against too-easy acceptance of the notion of "arrested development" (on this task noneducated adults were *not* equivalent to noneducated children), but it also suggests that some experiential factors other than formal Western-type schooling may further the switch from nonsemantic to semantic bases of classification.

In addition to mapping the way in which these different Kpelle populations actually grouped the items, Scribner asked each individual to explain the reason why he put particular items together in one group. Here, differences among the adult populations became very marked. High-schoolers almost always gave a category label to their groups ("these are clothes") or expressed their category status by some statement referring to a common attribute of the group members ("you can hunt with these"). In sharp contrast, 70 percent of the bush villagers gave reasons that had nothing to do with the properties of the objects they were grouping; most of their explanations were arbitrary statements, such as "I like them this way" or "my sense told me to do it this way." The transitional village residents (cash workers and road villagers) gave fewer arbitrary reasons than the bush villagers, but fell well below the high-schoolers in citing a common attribute or giving a class name; a common mode of response was to link together items in the group through their different uses—for example, an explanation given for putting net, pot, pepper, okra, and peanut in one group was "the net is for fishing, the okra and peanut are cooked in the pot.

Practically no 6- to 8-year-old could explain his groupings; the overwhelming majority of the children responded to the experimenter's question by repeating the instructions ("you told me to group them") or citing personal authority ("I wanted to do it that way, so I did"). They showed no recognition of the fact that the properties of the materials themselves might provide a basis for dividing the items into groups. Little improvement was shown by the 10- to 14-year-olds who had not been to school, but nearly half of the older children who *had* been to school cited a common attribute of the items or the class name when giving their reason for grouping, and less than one out of five gave an arbitrary reason.

While nonliterate adult villagers and 10- to 14-year-old schoolchildren were quite similar in their *practical* classifying activities, they were very dissimilar in the verbal explanations they gave for these activities: younger people with schooling reflect the category nature of their groupings in the way they describe them; villagers without schooling do not. To make the generalization even stronger, we may say that the only two populations in Scribner's study who made explicit use of class names or common attributes as justification for the classifications were the educated populations. Since a substantial part of Greenfield's evidence for school–nonschool differences in classifying had to do with the way various groups *verbalized* their sorting activities, it may be useful to make a distinction, in the future, between the way individuals operate with things (their actual sorting operations) and the way they describe their own operations. In the study just reported, the most robust effects of education appeared to be on verbalization.

Summary

When we moved on from grand theory to a review of studies on classification processes among traditional people, we found that the terms frequently used in the psychological literature to classify thought processes are somewhat deficient. *Abstract* and *concrete* have been used in a rather loose manner to designate a number of different operations, which do not always co-vary: the particular attribute the individual selects as the basis for grouping; whether he uses this attribute consistently to form all groups in an experimental task; whether he switches from one basis of classification to another; and how he describes and explains the classes he makes. With these many meanings of the terms in mind, it is clear that experimental findings do not allow the conclusion that in general the thinking of any group of people is, or is not, abstract.

We have seen that the attribute selected as the basis for grouping is sensitive to the nature of the materials worked with: how familiar they are (rice versus geometric stimuli), the content domain from which they are drawn (animals versus plants), and the form in which they are presented (objects versus pictures). Although selection of taxonomic class membership as a grouping principle has traditionally (within psychology) been considered the hallmark of abstract thinking, we have seen that this is not an all-or-none affair—the degree to which taxonomic class properties control sorting behavior seems to vary with the saliency of other grouping principles (how items from different classes are functionally related to each other, for example). Does this leave us, then, with an unassimilable relativism? In other words, does it all depend on the materials and the situations? With the information now on hand, we would suggest that classifying operations do seem to change in certain ways with exposure to Western or modern living experiences. Taxonomic class membership seems to play a more dominating role as the basis for grouping items when people move from isolated village life to towns more affected by commerce and the exchange of people and things. Attendance at a Western-type school accentuates this switchover to taxonomic grouping principles. But schooling seems to affect even more than this: attendance at school apparently encourages an approach to classification tasks that incorporates a search for a rule—for a principle that can generate the answers. At the same time, schooling seems to promote an awareness of the fact that alternative rules are possible—one might call this a formal approach to the task in which the individual searches for and selects from the several possibilities a rule of solution. Finally, the one unambiguous finding in the studies to date is that schooling (and only schooling) contributes to the way in which people describe and explain their own mental operations. This last fact suggests an important distinction that should be made in future research—that is, a differentiation between what people *do* and what people *say* they do.

chapter 6　*Culture,*
Learning,
and Memory

A great deal of cross-cultural psychological research is based on notions and theories about non-Western thinking that are centered about a *deficiency hypothesis.* This line of thinking typically engenders generalizations such as the following: "In respect to such-and-such a cognitive skill, X tribe fails to perform as well as (American) (Genevan) (English) groups." But when we turn to the area of memory, the picture is reversed. The severest critics of "primitive mentality" unite in extolling the superlative quality of primitive *memory,* and find Europeans wanting in comparison.

An early seventeenth-century observer (Evreux, 1613) of the Tupinamba tribe in Brazil reported admiringly that "they have excellent memories and they always remember what they have seen or heard and they can tell you all the circumstances of place, time and persons, the things said or done." Three centuries later the same point was made by Elizabeth Bowen (1954), who recounted the displeasure and consternation of her Nigerian hosts at her inability to remember the names of local plants, which every six-year-old in the village had long since committed to memory. Additional evidence of African memory abilities is provided by Bartlett (1932). He ran a miniature memory test on a Swazi cowherder who one year earlier had been tangentially involved in a series of cattle transactions. The herder was able to recall identifying marks as well as the price paid for each cow in pounds, shillings, and pence, with almost no errors.

Both Bowen and Bartlett attribute the memory feats of their informants to their great interest in plants (or cows). The cowherder's feat of memory seems outstanding only because what is socially important to him is irrelevant to the Western observer, who therefore finds a good memory for cows and plants highly unusual. We might, according to this theory, expect a Swazi herder to be equally astounded if he encountered a Los Angeles ten-year-old trading baseball cards with a friend. The intricate recall of players, teams, batting averages, and relative standing that the successful card-trader requires would seem virtually impossible to the Swazi cowherder, to whom all baseball players look alike!

This commonsense explanation of how social relevance and interest affect *what* is remembered was neatly demonstrated in an experiment by Deregowski (1970).

He was struck by the different significances attached to time in traditional rural settings as compared with urban settings and reasoned that memory for time concepts should reflect this difference in cultural valuation. His subjects were members of the Tumbuka tribe in Zambia and were drawn from two populations assumed to reflect the greatest contrast in the role that time measurement played in their daily lives. The first group was composed of primary school students living in town: schools adhere to timetables, discourage lateness, and emphasize dates, and the urban environment in general requires conformity with time schedules. The daily life of a village dweller, however, is relatively independent of time considerations: there are no timepieces. Activities follow their own rhythm and are not governed by set schedules. For his test material, Deregowski composed a short story containing eight items of numerical information, four of which dealt with various aspects of time. After each subject heard the story, he was asked questions that revealed how much of the numerical information was retained. As hypothesized, rural people were considerably inferior to the schoolboys in their retention of time information, but were equivalent in their recall of three of the four nontemporal concepts. Further analyses of the data showed that these differences between groups arose because the rural people handled the nontemporal concepts better than they handled the temporal concepts. As Deregowski observes, even "recall of digits is not independent of their significance and . . . such significance is culturally determined" (1970, p. 40).

The selectivity of memory is, of course, a well-documented phenomenon within Western cultures (a classic reference is Rapaport, 1950), and to the extent that it obtains among Africans and other non-Westerners, we have still further evidence of certain universal aspects of mental functioning. But, in addition to testimony about how well nonliterate people recall certain things, there have been repeated suggestions in the literature that cultural characteristics make a difference in the *way* things are recalled. Bartlett (1932), for example, contrasted two types of remembering —an active process, in which past experience and information is reconstructed for the purpose at hand, and rote memory, a recapitulation of what has occurred, which simply runs it off in the original temporal sequence (a kind of serial memorizing). He hypothesizes that rote memory is the preferred memory technique of nonliterate peoples:

> According to the general theory of remembering which has been put forward, there is a low level type of recall which comes as nearly as possible to what is often called rote recapitulation. It is characteristic of a mental life having relatively few interests, all somewhat concrete in character and no one of which is dominant (p. 264).

Another hypothesis about memory in non-literate societies stresses the special practices and techniques that such cultures must develop in order to guarantee the transmission of information from one generation to the next. The "wisdom of the elders" can only survive in the memory of the living; there is no book to look things up in, and thus the information held in mind by individual members of the culture is a valuable asset for the whole community. D'Azevedo (1962, p. 13) reports that among the Gola of western Liberia, "an elder with a poor memory or whose old people told him nothing is a 'small boy' among the elders and might well be looked upon with contempt by younger persons." And a contemporary saying among South American Indians sadly observes that "when an old man dies, a whole library burns." Because knowledge resides in living memory, oral societies have produced special mnemonic devices to aid in the preservation of the cultural store. Such at least is the intriguing thesis of the phiologist-historian Havelock (1963), who considers the epic poem such a device and analyzes how its special features of rhyme, rhythm, and repetition contribute to its function as the "oral encyclopedia" of the social, material, and historical aspects of the culture. From the point of view of our interests, this thesis suggests that remembering in traditional societies may rely, to a considerable extent, on special memory supports and devices.

Studies in Free Recall

In the past few years, a series of studies of memory have been carried out in Africa by Cole, Gay, Glick, and Sharp (1971) as a means to deciding among various explanations of the observations we have been reporting.

Their first concern was to find an experimental tool or set of tools that would be appropriate to the study of memory processes across cultures and that could reveal *how* the people were going about the memory task. They began by seeking some procedure that could at one and the same time permit either rote learning or active reorganization of the material to occur, in order to test Bartlett's hypothesis about culture and memory.

The free-recall experiment, originally used by Bousfield (1953) for the study of organizational processes in memory, seemed an excellent candidate. A free-recall experiment is extremely easy to administer. A subject is presented a series of items, one at a time, and is told that he must try to learn them so that he can recall them later. The list can then be repeated as many times as the experimenter wishes.

Free recall is so named because the subject is free to remember in any manner he chooses. The way in which he orders the lists when recalling them in this unconstrained fashion gives important insight into the organizational mechanisms of memory. For instance, if he recalls items in the same order in which they were presented, we could characterize his performance as "rote." He might also tend to recall items in clusters, or groups based on some common category. Clustering by taxonomic category is a mode of organization prevalent among older schoolchildren in the United States (Bousfield, 1953; Cole, Frankel & Sharp, 1972; and many others). But it is possible to analyze freely recalled material in a variety of ways so as to evaluate alternative hypotheses about the way in which to-be-remembered material is organized.

As a starting point for the research, sets of items were constructed using standard anthropological eliciting techniques.* This preliminary work assured the experimenters that the test material was familiar and that the subjects knew its linguistic structure.

Table 6–1 contains two lists of items used in several studies of cultural variations in memory performance. The first list is termed

Table 6–1. List of Items Used in Kpelle Recall Studies

Clusterable	Nonclusterable
Plate	Bottle
Calabash	Nickle
Pot	Chicken feather
Pan	Box
Cup	Battery
	Animal horn
Potato	Stone
Onion	Book
Banana	Candle
Orange	Cotton
Coconut	Hard mat
	Rope
Cutlass	Nail
Hoe	Cigarette
Knife	Stick
File	Grass
Hammer	Pot
	Knife
Trousers	Orange
Singlet	Shirt
Headtie	
Shirt	
Hat	

*The data reported here are taken from studies among the Kpelle of Liberia (Cole et al., 1971).

"clusterable" because of the obvious division into easily identifiable semantic categories; the second is termed "nonclusterable" because it was constructed so as to provide minimal groupings into taxonomic categories.

The experimental attack focused on the types of persons, verbal instructions, and material conditions that could reasonably be expected to affect the rate of learning and structuring of recall under free-recall procedures. One variation involved the nature of the stimulus materials. A point that many observers of African learning seem to emphasize is the presumed concreteness of African thought. It was reasoned, then, that if people were shown the objects on the list instead of having the names of the objects read to them, recall and clustering would be augmented.

A second variation involved the nature of the lists. American evidence indicates that clusterable lists are easier to learn and are better recalled, in general, than lists whose components belong to disparate classes. If the Kpelle rely on rote memory rather than on the taxonomic organization of the list, they ought to recall both lists equally well.

Another variable that has been found to affect recall is the arrangement of items in a clusterable list. If the items are *not* randomly arranged, but rather are presented in blocks (with all items in a given class succeeding each other), clustering and recall are enhanced for American college students (Cofer, 1967).

In the first experimental series, Kpelle subjects were selected from three age groups: 6 to 8 years, 10 to 14 years, and 18 to 50 years. Within the first two age groups, comparisons were made between nonschooled children and children in the first grade and second to fourth grades, respectively. Since it is very rare to find an educated tribal adult, the experiments did not include educated adult groups.

In order to make cross-cultural comparisons, data were collected from children in southern California who are primarily white and are from middle-class homes. Although this population is clearly not optimal (a wide range of socioeconomic and ethnic backgrounds should be investigated), it was used because of its availability.

The standard experimental procedure used in these tasks was to present the test list and ask for recall on five successive trials. The outcome of this series of experiments, as well as of several additional experiments, can be summarized in capsule form as follows:

1. As American children grow older, the number of words recalled and the rate at which the list is learned increase markedly; older Liberian Kpelle subjects recall only slightly more than younger subjects, and educated subjects recall slightly more than noneducated subjects. Most striking is the fact that, on the whole, learning is very slow for Liberian subjects; only a very few more words are recalled on the fifth presentation of the list than were recalled on the first presentation.

2. Clusterable lists are learned a little more easily by all the Kpelle groups, and by all the American groups as well.

3. The American children, especially those 10 years old and older, cluster their recall—that is, items from the same taxonomic category are said together—but the Kpelle show little or no semantic clustering.

4. The Kpelle subjects all recall objects better than spoken words, but so do the Americans.

How are we to interpret these results? Taken at face value, they tell us that we should seriously question reports of fabulous memory power among traditional nonliterate peoples. Not only were the performances of our Kpelle groups poor when compared with American groups of similar ages, but educated children tended to perform better than their nonliterate age-mates. This result is just the opposite of what we would expect if lack of literacy fostered memory.

With respect to the structure of the recall performance, we might be tempted to conclude that the absence of taxonomic clustering is evidence for Bartlett's hypothesis about a "low-level type of recall" among traditional peoples. However, analyses of these data lend no support at all to the idea that the Kpelle depend upon rote recapitulation as a structuring principle. If they did, we should have found that the order in which the words were recalled would have corresponded closely with the order in which the words were presented. But it did not. Correlation coefficents were calculated for the two orders, and in no case did the Kpelle correlations deviate significantly from zero. So much for rote recapitulation!

Had the experimental series stopped at this point, our conclusions would have had to be that in a laboratory experimental situation, which makes arbitrary demands on memory, African memory (as measured by free-recall performance among the Kpelle) is worse than American memory, and that literacy improves recall rather than the other way around. However, to have stopped here would have left this investigation open to a host of criticisms.

Some of the most obvious hypotheses about possible sources of difficulty for the Kpelle in this kind of experimental situation come readily to mind. Perhaps the people did not understand what was required of them; perhaps they were indifferent to the task and did not try to remember; perhaps they were deliberately playing dumb. Instead of reviewing the work that was aimed at evaluating this kind of interpretation (the interested reader should refer to Cole et al., 1971), we will describe a line of research that we think offers greater promise of helping us understand the complex antecedents of good memory performance.

We felt that the proper object of this research was to find out what kinds of conditions are required for Liberian subjects to show good memory skills in an experimental situation. Our guiding hypothesis was that something about the way in which free-recall experiments are usually conducted failed to provide subjects in Liberia with the needed reminders of the material that had been presented.

We began our new line of investigation with a vague notion that the performance of the Kpelle subjects would be improved if the categories latent in the clusterable list were somehow signaled by an object in the real world. Thus we arranged a situation in which the objects shown to our subjects were associated with chairs. Perhaps, we hypothesized, concreteness is not an attribute of the material to be learned, but lies in the relation of this material to some external recall cue.

The experimenter stood behind four chairs with the subject in front, facing him. Behind the experimenter was a table containing the objects to be remembered. As the names of the objects were read they were held up one at a time over chairs, and then the subject was asked to recall the items (but not which chair they were associated with). The procedure was repeated for five trials.

The presentation of items followed a different pattern for each of three different groups of 10- to 14-year-old schoolchildren. For one group, items from a given category were all held over one particular chair on each trial; thus each category was assigned one chair. For the second group, items were assigned at random to the four chairs, with the assignment remaining the same for each trial. For the third group, all items were held over the same chair; the other three chairs were not used.

The chair procedure produced much higher recall, for all three groups, than any we had previously observed, making it appear that the fact of having a concrete reminder is more critical for good recall than the particular form the reminder takes. The next problem was to determine whether this "reminder" notion could be extended to other kinds of cues besides physical ones. A question of particular importance from a pedagogical point of view is whether some means of *verbal* cuing could augment recall. Could we teach our subjects to remember better using mechanisms less unwieldy than chairs?

In an initial attempt to use verbal cues, subjects were read the standard clusterable list and recall was measured under five conditions.

In three of these conditions, subjects were cued with the names of the categories in the list. At some point in the experimental procedure the experimenter said to the subject, "These things are *clothing, tools, food* and *utensils.*" One group heard this statement when the list was presented, another after the list had been read but just before it was to be recalled, and a third group heard it at both presentation and recall. A fourth experimental group served as a control and received no cuing at all. Finally, a fifth group of subjects were not cued in the manner we have described but were instead *required* to recall the items by category (we refer to this group as the "constrained" group). At the time of recall, the experimenter would say, for example, "Tell me all the *clothing* you remember." After the subject had named all the clothing items he could remember, the experimenter would ask for each of the other categories in turn. This procedure was followed on the first four trials, but on the fifth trial, without warning, the subject was simply told to name as many of the items as he could.

Comparison of the first four groups indicated that simply cuing the subjects with the category names at time of presentation or recall had little effect on either the amount remembered or clustering. There were no significant differences among groups, and performance was comparable to that obtained in the standard oral free-recall presentation situation.

The results from the fifth group, whose recall was constrained to systematic retrieval by category, were quite different. The number of words recalled on the first four trials was extremely high and, most important, it remained high on the fifth "free" trial. Clustering was forced to be perfect for the first four trials with this group, but on the fifth trial clustering remained high and was comparable to the performance of American schoolchildren. It appeared that good recall and highly organized recall could be induced through sufficiently explicit verbal instruction and training.

This is an important result when coupled with demonstrations such as the improvement of recall through the use of explicit, external memory aids (like the chairs). It tells us that we cannot speak of "good" and "bad" memory as if memory were a unitary process. Rather, we need to analyze overall memory performance into its constituent subprocesses and then determine how these processes are brought to bear on a given memory task.

For example, the fact that the constrained-recall condition greatly enhanced recall from the very first trial strongly suggests that many more of the test items were "in the subjects' heads" than they could recall. The constrained group was treated just like the other groups up to the point where they had to start telling the experimenter what they could remember. Since the constraints were introduced *after* all the items had been presented, these results suggest that the difficulty our Kpelle subjects experience is one of making stored material accessible (or, alternatively, of retrieving material that is stored in memory). It could be said that the constrained recall made stored material accessible and in the process taught the subject retrieval habits that carried over to the unconstrained-recall trial.

Having achieved such effects in our standard experimental situation, we next wanted to find out whether Kpelle would routinely use efficient retrieval processes on their own in a more natural memory situation.

In most previous research, the paradigm for the study of memory in naturalistic situations has involved recall of stories. The classic research in this area is described in Bartlett's book (1932) to which we made reference earlier. Bartlett's work, while interesting, could not completely solve our needs. We wanted to know how the skills involved in normally occurring recall (which usually involves meaningfully connected material) make contact with the skills involved in the experimental memory task (which involves disconnected material).

We chose a middle course, which we think permits us to link recall for connected and disconnected material. The basic strategy we adopted was to provide a range of story contexts in which to present the 20 basic clusterable items from Table 6-1. At one extreme, no context at all was provided (our basic oral-presentation procedure was repeated); at the other extreme, items were embedded in a story context in which each item was meaningfully linked to a neighboring item. Two alternative forms of these stories were the following:

STORY 1. A chief had a beautiful daughter, and many young men wanted to marry her. Each of them brought many presents for the girl and left them with the chief. One brought (name the tools). Another brought (name the foods). Another brought (name the utensils). And another brought (name the clothing). *What things did the girl receive? Which young man should get the girl? Why?*

STORY 2. A very handsome man, who happened to be a bogeyman, came to town one day and met a beautiful girl. The girl did not know he was a bogeyman and agreed to marry him. On the night they married, she discovered he was a bogeyman. He told her she must come with him to his farm, but she said to wait a bit while she got her things together. She knew where the bogeyman's farm was, and so she put many things on the ground in her house to show her people the way to reach his farm. She put her *plate* first, since she always ate at home. Then she put the bogeyman's *singlet* to show that he took her away. Then she put a *pot* to show that he took her first in the direction of her family's kitchen behind the house. Then she put a *knife* to show that they went past the woodcarver's house. Next was a *headtie* showing that they passed the store where she bought it. Next was an *onion* to show they passed the market, and a *cup* to show they passed the table where they sell palm wine. Next was a *hammer* to show they passed the house being built on that trail. She then put down a *hat* to show that the house belongs to the teacher. Next was a *file* to show they passed the blacksmith's kitchen. Then came a *banana* to show they took the road with the banana trees, a *shirt* to show they passed the place where they wash clothes, and a *calabash* to show they passed the place where they get drinking water. Then she put an *orange* to show that they took the trail with the orange tree, and a *cutlass* showed that the trail was newly cut. Then came the *trousers* to show they passed the weaver's farm, and a *coconut* to show they took the road with the coconut tree on it. Then came a *hoe* to show that she was on a farm, and a *potato* to show that it was a potato farm, and finally a *pan* to show that she was at the kitchen at the farm. The girl's people saw all these things and understood where she had gone and came and rescued her. They caught the bogeyman and killed him. *Tell all the things she put on the ground and their meaning so that if you were the girl's family, you could find the girl.*

The stories were read by the experimenter who wrote down the subject's responses in the standard manner. Then a tape recorder was turned on to record the subject's version of the story.

The upshot of this experiment was that the way in which the to-be-recalled items fit into the story almost perfectly determined the organization of recall. For Story 1, there was a very strong tendency to recall the items by category. For Story 2, just the opposite relation held: items were recalled more or less in the order in which they fit into the story, and category clustering was at a minimum. And, when items were clustered by category in response to Story 1, the order within each cluster was found to have no relation to the order presented in the narrative, a piece of evidence indicating that in recall the subjects were reconstructing the material on the basis of category membership rather than reeling it off by rote. This experiment, which examines recall processes in a situation close to those naturally encountered in the culture, dispels the notion that memory mechanisms among the Kpelle are like serial automata, which run themselves off on all occasions. Rather, it shows recall processes to be flexible and responsive to the structure provided in the to-be-remembered material, even when this structure is based on taxonomic categories.

Organizing and Other Memory Techniques

Since we have now established that taxonomic structure is *sometimes* used by the Kpelle to direct recall, we can return to the question of why it was not used with the word list in the original free-recall situation. Instead of general explanations couched in terms of good and bad memory, or "the ability to categorize," we now want to pose the question: What kinds of categorization is a traditional Kpelle person likely to apply to the free-recall task? What conditions control whether or not a category structure is used?

There are several possibilities. While Kpelle *can* utilize semantic categories, this may not be their preferred mode of organizing material. Perhaps they would make greater use of a structure reflecting their own preferred basis for grouping. Perhaps the difficulty arises because the free-recall situation requires the subject to reorder the material (organize it) *on his own initiative*—it has to occur to him to do it; if the thought does not occur, no reordering (structuring) will occur. (In the story-telling task, the story fixed the order that the subjects utilized, and under constrained recall, the experimenter told the subject to reorder the material on recall.)

Each of these possibilities was investigated in a separate study by Scribner (unpublished). In the first study, subjects were required to sort 25 familiar objects into groups that "went together," putting at least three items in a group. Two sets of objects were selected paralleling as closely as possible the items in the clusterable and nonclusterable lists of the original free-recall study (see Table 6–1). After the sorting had been completed, the objects were mixed up and the subject was asked to group them again exactly as he had before. This classifying activity was continued until the individual had sorted the items into identical groups on two successive trials. (This procedure and a description of the kinds of groupings that were made was described in greater detail in Chapter 5.) Once a stable way of grouping had been achieved and recorded, the objects were removed and the subject was asked to recall as many as he could. In this way, subjects were given an opportunity to organize material according to their own preferred criteria, and the experimenter had exact information about the nature and composition of each individual's groups. It was then possible to analyze the recall output, not only in terms of how well it reflected the semantic categories the experimenter had built into the list, but how well it reflected the subject's own categories (groups).

This study was run with four adult populations, selected to represent various degrees of involvement in modern institutions (high school students, cash workers, rice farmers in a road village, and rice farmers in an isolated village far in the bush).

Perhaps the outstanding finding was that all of these Kpelle people—literate and nonliterate, cash worker and farmer, road villager and bush villager—did make use of their own groupings to structure their recall. Their recall order followed their own-group ordering to a greater extent than might be expected by chance. This common technique of using structure to guide recall is all the more interesting because different structures were involved for the different groups. The structures were most different for the two population groups at the extreme ends of the modernization scale; high school students relied almost exclusively on taxonomic categories as the basis for grouping, and bush farmers made little use of this principle. This does not mean, however, that the nature of the groupings had no effect on the amount of recall clustering: recall cluster scores in general paralleled the scores for taxonomic groupings—the high school students on top, followed closely by the cash workers and then by the two farming groups. Moreover, there was a marked decline in recall clustering, among all populations, for the list that was put together out of unrelated items, although this list, too, had been given forced organization. It would appear, then, that there is a relation between the kind of organizing principle used to group material and its efficiency as a guide to recall.

This study provided evidence that Kpelle people do take advantage of prior organization of material when confronted with a recall task; their recall is not haphazard, nor is it unrelated to what has gone before. In this procedure, however, subjects were again *required* to work on the material and reorder it. The question still remains: Do Kpelle spontaneously reorganize material as an aid to memory? Scribner's second study suggests that the answer is "rarely."

A free study situation was devised, patterned after that employed by Moely, Olson, Halwes, and Flavell (1969) in their investigation of the development of memorizing techniques among American school children. Forty high-schoolers and 40 villagers in traditional (non–cash) occupations were tested. With some variation in the manner of presentation of the material (which need not concern us here), all subjects were given a 2-minute period to study 24 familiar objects. Experimenters recorded what the subjects did to try to remember the material, with special attention to whether they made any attempt to divide the object array into meaningful and more memorizable units, whether they engaged in verbal rehearsal, and whether they tried to test themselves before the experimenter asked for recall.

Half the subjects were given broad instructions to "do anything you want to help you remember," and half were given additional instructions to carry the objects to another table "in any way that will help you remember." The instructions to "carry" the material were introduced in the belief that forced handling of the material would encourage individuals to regroup or rearrange the items. This hypothesis, however, proved to be mistaken with respect to the villagers: only 3 people out of 20 attempted to lay the objects out in groups after they had carried them to a new table, only 2 more than in the no-carry condition. Most of them laid out the objects haphazardly or heaped them up; several tried to reconstitute the original order in which the experimenter had laid them out. High-schoolers did respond to the extra prodding of the carry instructions by breaking up the original order and regrouping the items—10 out of 20 subjects in this condition engaged in some grouping activities. Surprisingly, only 3 students in the corresponding no-carry condition spontaneously engaged in the reorganization of the material. It thus seems that spontaneous structuring of material as a deliberate aid to recall is not a common technique in the repertoire of traditional Kpelle adults and that it is less common among Kpelle students than it has been found to be among American students. Moely and associates found, for example, that even at the fifth-grade level, the majority of children spontaneously used category grouping of material as an aid to memory.

Although the villagers failed to regroup the material, they did engage in other memorizing techniques—almost all named the items and rehearsed the names during the study period; some demonstrated and described the functions of the items as well. Again, cultural differences in memorization do not seem to consist in the presence or absence of mnemonic techniques *in general*, but in the utilization of a specific technique—reorganization of to-be-remembered material. The question for future research is whether this particular device for learning and recall of material is tied directly to school learning experiences or whether it is responsive to other learning experience encountered in urban or modern life.

Summary

As we remarked at the outset of this chapter, the study of memory and culture began from a different set of premises from those that motivated the study of culture and other cognitive processes; memory was the one cognitive process said to be more highly developed in nonliterate than literate peoples.

Yet when we turn to the experimental evidence, we see no hint of a *general* superiority on the part of nonliterate peoples, nor do we encounter qualitatively different modes of remembering, such as the rote recapitulation method suggested by Bartlett.

One might suppose that anthropological reports of special mnemonic powers have been mistaken or exaggerated. A more likely explanation is that the anthropological reports are correct —their informants do in fact remember things that the anthropologists find it difficult or impossible to recall. But this performance is not reflective of greater powers of memory in *general*; rather it reflects the fact that the things a Philippine native or !Kung bushman finds easy to recall are different from the things the anthropologist finds easy to recall. In short, how well someone remembers a particular subject matter depends on the subject at hand. This was certainly Bartlett's idea when he attributed his subjects' impressive recall of details about cows and cow prices to the fact that cows are central to the lives of the people he was studying. In much the same way, we find our children's memory for baseball averages and the details of movie stars' lives unusual, if not exotic.

The experimental findings on memory certainly fit this general orientation. On those few occasions where differential recall of particular content has been studied (Deregowski, 1970; Nadel, 1937) dominant cultural themes—the things that people care about—have been found to have a strong influence on what is remembered.

But in the studies we have reported on the amount and organization of recall, wherever differences in memory are encountered, they show the nonliterate peoples to be performing more poorly than their literate, and generally more urban, counterparts. How are we to interpret these findings?

One conclusion we might come to is that the to-be-recalled materials in our experiment are not reflective of dominant cultural themes. Consequently, the subject cannot fit them into any pre-existing scheme of things. In the course of normal events, things are remembered because their natural contexts are organized in ways that matter to the individual and make sense in terms of his social experiences. Presumably, the experiment in which the items to be recalled were embedded in traditional-style folk stories provided the kind of structure that ordinarily serves to organize remembering, and in that situation we found the structure of recall matching the structure of the story.

But the more typical of our free-recall tasks failed to evoke any such natural structure. At least intuitively, one can see why this might be the case. Unlike most common memory situations, our experimental version of free recall uses material that is not connected grammatically. The items named are familiar, but the motivation to remember them comes from an arbitrary source, such as the desire to earn money or appear clever. The study by Scribner in which subjects sorted objects prior to recall shows that when organization is *required*, it is made use of for the purpose of recall, strengthening our belief that we have identified the important features controlling recall.

It appears that the cultural difference in memory performance tapped in the free-recall studies rests upon the fact that the more sophisticated (highly educated) subjects respond to the task by searching for and imposing a structure upon which to base their recall. Noneducated subjects are not likely to engage in such structure-imposing activity. When they do, or when the task itself gives structure to the material, cultural differences in performance are greatly reduced or eliminated.

The fact that we are studying a rather restricted domain of memory performance in the studies described here is unfortunate. But this should not detract from the potential significance of the results of such work. There is little doubt that success in school, among other things, requires of children that they learn to commit large amounts of initially unrelated material to memory. It is unfortunate that so little research on memory and culture can be reported; a wide variety of memory tasks are currently the sub-

ject of intense investigation in the United States, and their application in cross-cultural settings would put us in a position to
make stronger statements about the kinds of mnemonic skills fostered in traditional societies.

chapter 7 *Culture and Problem Solving*

No aspect of the relation between culture and cognition has a longer history or has produced more controversy than the question of whether the reasoning processes of preliterate peoples differ from those of industrialized peoples. For many years, popular and scientific views were in agreement that whatever other mental capacities primitive people might excel in, their capacities for sound reasoning and systematic thinking were surely deficient compared to "ours." The following statements, the first from an explorer, the second from a highly respected, early anthropologist are typical:

> The African Negro, or Bantu, does not think, reflect, or reason if he can help it. He has a wonderful memory, has great powers of observation and imitation, . . . and very many good qualities . . . but the reasoning and inventive faculties remain dormant. He readily grasps the present circumstances, adapts himself to them and provides for them; but a careful, thought out plan or a clever piece of induction is beyond him (Bentley, 1929, p. 26).

Between our clearness of separation of what is in the mind from
what is out of it, and the mental confusion of the lowest savage of
our own day, there is a vast interval (Tylor, 1865, p. 125).

In the twentieth century, Lucien Levy-Bruhl, whose ideas we
discussed briefly in Chapter 2, formulated a theory of primitive
thought that gave the argument the particular turn that has dominated it ever since. In his book, *How Natives Think*, first published in 1910, he characterized primitive thought as *prelogical*,
thereby stirring up a storm of controversy in the social sciences
about the relation between logic and thought. Levy-Bruhl's statements were construed to mean that primitive thinking is *illogical*,
and contenders lined up on either side of the debate over whether
such an allegation was justified with respect to any human thought.
In fact, however, Levy-Bruhl took great pains to point out that by
the term *prelogical* he did not mean antilogical or nonlogical. Nor
was he referring to a type of thought that was a forerunner of
Western logical thought. Rather, he maintained that he was simply
using the term to characterize a form of thinking, rare among us
but dominant among primitives, that is governed by what he
called a "law of participation." Under this law, phenomena have
the attribute of being "themselves" and yet partaking of other
phenomena as well. This kind of thinking, Levy-Bruhl claimed,
stands in contrast to the dominant form of Western thinking,
which is governed by the logical *law of contradiction*, under which
a phenomenon cannot be both itself and not itself at the same
time. He cited the following beliefs as instances of prelogical
thinking: a group of Brazilian Indians claim that they are also
parrots; Bororo believe that portraits possess some of the qualities of life of their models; a village man attacked by a snake
feels himself responsible for the death of a child in the next
village.

Anthropologists in general rejected Levy-Bruhl's theory that
primitive thinking fails to reflect the laws of Western logic. He
himself had made it clear that he was talking only about the general laws governing *collective representations* (roughly, beliefs)
of primitive peoples, not those governing the everyday behavior
of individuals in such societies. Boas (1911) was quick to follow
up the implications of this approach, noting that "if we disregard
the thinking of the individual in our society and pay attention

only to current beliefs . . . we should reach the conclusion that the same attitudes prevail among ourselves that are characteristic of primitive man" (p. 128).

A. F. C. Wallace (1962) took another line of attack. He pointed out that if primitive peoples thought according to a radically different rule of logic, man would probably be extinct. Imagine what would happen, says Wallace, if a primitive hunter were to reason thus: a rabbit has four legs; that animal has four legs; therefore, that animal is a rabbit. In his own work (Wallace, 1970), he has demonstrated that kinship terminologies and other concept domains have underlying logical systems. He is joined in this work by other anthropologists in a new discipline, cognitive anthropology, which attempts to delineate the logical structure of primitive classification systems—an enterprise that is somewhat like a mirror image of what Levy-Bruhl attempted.

Few would disagree with the contention that many of the beliefs of preliterate people differ strikingly from ours. One example of such a difference—the belief in lightning magic among the Kpelle—was given in Chapter 1. The critical issue is what to make of such instances. What does knowledge about a belief tell us of the reasoning processes that underlie it? We would maintain that it is not possible to make valid inferences about thought processes —that is, about the specific mechanisms producing a particular behavior or beliefs—solely on the basis of evidence about the beliefs of groups or individuals. If Levy-Bruhl was correct, we can not be sure of it using only the data he presents; if he was incorrect, we could not know it if we relied on the characteristics of belief systems and conceptual systems as our evidence. Even behavioral evidence drawn from everyday observation may be inconclusive. Consider the following example (taken from Morgan, 1877): A man sees black clouds on the horizon and says it is going to rain. Did he make an inference, or did he simply remember the association, black clouds → rain? But let us complicate the example. Suppose that a man uses instruments to measure wind velocity and barometric pressure. A certain combination of wind velocity and barometric pressure is observed, and he says it is going to rain. Did he make an inference? It would seem more likely than in the first case, but it is still possible that he simply remembered this case from an earlier experience. In fact, without

specific kinds of prior knowledge about the person and the circumstances involved, it is impossible to determine whether a particular conclusion is a remembered instance from the past or an
example of inference based on present circumstances. Hence no
reliable evidence about the logic of the inference can be obtained
from such anecdotes.

Clearly Levy-Bruhl is in an impossible position when it comes
to making inferences about thought processes from information
about beliefs, but so are his critics. Each can point to the reasonableness of his own explanation, but for any given instance,
neither party can really determine what processes were involved.

As it turns out, these methodological difficulties in the study of
thinking are not peculiar to cross-cultural research. They are at
the heart of psychology's most serious scientific problems and
have often been the touchstone for evaluating the scientific merit
of one or another school of psychology. In the early days, the new
laboratories of psychology were interested in studying thought
processes, and they placed considerable reliance on the method of
introspection—on securing reports from the subject about what
was going on in his mind while he attempted to solve certain problems put before him by the experimenter. Certain disadvantages
of this methodology were obvious from the outset: How can one
study thinking in children or animals, for example? Other disadvantages soon became obvious: How can one resolve disputes as
to whether there are thought processes that are not represented
in words or imagery in the mind of the self-observer? Questions
of this kind contributed to the conviction of militant behaviorists
that the very subject matter of *thinking* was unfit for psychological study. Not only the method of introspection, but the topic of
thinking itself dropped out of many experimental laboratories
in the twenties, thirties, and forties. The Gestalt psychologists
(Duncker, 1945; Köhler, 1925; Wertheimer, 1959) kept the problem alive during this period and made many valuable and original
contributions, but it was not until recently that thought again became a respectable area of research for experimental psychologists
of various theoretical persuasions.

The return to the study of thinking has been accompanied by
some conceptual progress and some new investigative tools, which
are helpful in cross-cultural study. There is now agreement at a

general level among psychologists about what is meant by *thinking*, although there is little agreement about how thought processes operate. With some difference in emphasis, most definitions would be compatible with Bartlett's (1958) statement that thinking is an extension of the evidence (present in the stimulus material or in memory) to produce something new: "It is the use of information about something present to get somewhere else." Bruner's phrase, "going beyond the information given," is another general statement of this view of thinking.

The basic idea underlying these and many other contemporary definitions of thinking is that its outcome should be some reorganization of the evidence in a way that is new for the one doing the thinking (others may have achieved the solution before, but its achievement for a given person will still represent a genuine act of thinking). If a person solved a problem solely by recall—by repetition of something previously learned—we would not call that thinking. We would be more inclined to consider this an instance of remembering. If a person solved a problem entirely on the basis of trial and error, we would be more likely to speak of his performance as learning rather than thinking. Thus, definitions of thinking imply that the subject is actively engaged with the evidence in order to reach a new end point.

Another feature of contemporary thinking about thinking is that it is not identified with logic. The relation between reasoning processes and those processes formalized in logical models is considered a question to be resolved by investigation rather than one to be settled by definition (Henle, 1962).

Finally, the emphasis on separating remembered conclusions from reasoned conclusions as a basic part of the definition of thinking has led to a strong emphasis on research that involves the solution of some problem the person has not previously experienced. Often this requirement means that the problem will appear somewhat unusual, especially to people for whom the whole idea of an artificially arranged problem is foreign.

With this background material in hand, we can review some of the data that are relevant to the question of culture and problem solving. Unfortunately, in our own country research on problem solving is rather sparse and has been focused on a limited number of problems. Even this range is not yet reflected in cross-cultural studies.

Conservation

The largest single body of cross-cultural studies on problem solving deals with Jean Piaget's concept of *conservation*. In its various forms, the notion of conservation has to do with the grasp of an object's *identity* under diverse changes of appearance. In one sense, the attainment of an identity concept can be considered a problem in concept-formation, or classification. David Elkind (1969), for example, points out that all concept formation is an attempt to deal with variability in the environment, and that such variability is of two major types. The first, and the one considered in our discussion of classification (Chapter 5), has to do with the variation *between* things, what Bruner refers to as "equivalence grouping"—considering dissimilar things similar for the purposes at hand. A second type is variability *within* things: "A young tree and a child both grow, a block of ice melts, a house gets painted and a car gets dented. All of these variations of form, of state, and of appearance occur within a given thing" (Elkind, pp. 172–173). This is the kind of variation with which Piaget has long been concerned—how one grasps as the "same" a thing that undergoes drastic transformations in physical properties.

Although Piagetian conservation does represent a type of concept formation in the sense described, most psychologists deal with his work as studies in the development of intelligence, or *logical operations*. This treatment derives from Piaget's theoretical framework, in which he views cognitive development as the construction of successively more complex systems of different types. Because Piaget's conceptual framework is *sui generis*, we feel that to a large extent a decision as to where and under what headings to review his work is somewhat arbitrary. Following what seems to be the more conventional approach, we have chosen this chapter on thinking as the place to take up the cross-cultural work devoted to his hypotheses. (For an excellent summary of Piaget's theory, see Ginsburg and Opper, 1969.)

The reference experiment on conservation is depicted in Figure 7–1. In each of the panels a different kind of material is used (beads, water, clay) to study different forms of conservation (number, volume, and amount). The experiment proceeds in an analogous fashion for each kind of material. For example, a 5-year-old subject is initially presented with two rows of beads

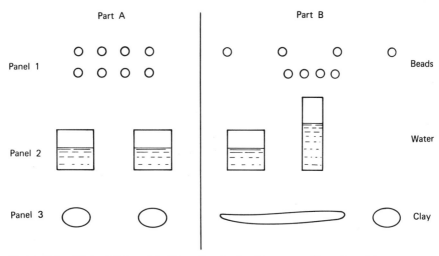

Figure 7-1. Materials used in Piagetian tests of conservation. *Panel 1,* arrangements of beads used to study conservation of *number; Panel 2,* containers of liquid used to study conservation of *volume; Panel 3,* clay used to study conservation of *amount.*

(Part A, Panel 1) of identical length and identical spacing. He is asked whether there are the same number of beads in the two rows, and he quickly agrees that there are. The spacing of one of the two rows of beads is then reduced so that it is shorter than the other row (Part B, Panel 1). Again the child is questioned: Do the two rows have the same number of beads? Which row has more beads? The child typically states that the longer row has more beads; that is, *the number of the set is not conserved when the length of the set is transformed.* An older child (say, 8 years old) will not be fooled by the change in the length of the set; he is therefore considered to have mastered the concept of number conservation.

The same kind of change occurs when the problem is presented in different forms. In Panel 2 of Figure 7–1, the question is whether or not the volumes of water in two beakers (Part A, Panel 2) are still judged equal when the water in one of the beakers is poured into a new beaker of a very different shape (Part B, Panel 2). In Panel 3, the question is whether the amount of clay is judged to be the same in spite of transformations in its shape.

For all of these problems Piaget has found a fixed sequence of development (although the exact age at which the child moves from one part of the sequence to the next varies from child to child and it is possible for the child to be at one stage with respect to *number* and another stage with respect to *volume*). It is this idea, that the developing child must go through a specifiable series of changes in the cognitive operations he has mastered, that makes Piaget's theory so attractive to study cross-culturally. The challenge that it poses is quite specific: Is the developmental sequence that Piaget has observed in Geneva, and that many investigators have observed in the United States, truly universal, or does it depend in some way on the early, culture-specific, experiences of the child? For example, it is often noted that children begin to manifest conservation (of number, volume, etc.) at about 6 to 7 years of age. This is the same age at which many children are beginning to attend school and learn to read; it may be that what moves the child from one mode of operation to another is specific skills acquired in connection with reading and writing, not some universal feature of human development.

One of the more extensive investigations of the development of conservation has been carried out by Greenfield (Bruner, Olver, and Greenfield, 1966). Her studies were done in Senegal, West Africa, among several groups of subjects, most of whom were members of the Wolof tribe. Greenfield chose the Wolof because children from this tribe could be found not only in traditional villages in the bush, but in villages where Western-style schooling (conducted in French) had been introduced, and in the cosmopolitan capital city of Dakar, where instruction was also in French for those attending school. This made it possible for her to study the roles of urbanization and education, as well as of age, in the development of conservation.

The first task studied by Greenfield is similar to that depicted in Figure 7–1, Panel 2. The child was given two beakers of identical shape and asked to equalize the water levels in them. The water of one beaker was then poured into a taller, thinner beaker, causing the water level to rise, and the child was asked whether the two different-shaped beakers (the new one and one of the old ones) contained the same amount of water, and if not, which beaker contained more. The results of this experiment carried out on several different groups of children are shown in Figure 7–2. The figure shows that by the age of 11 to 13 years, all children who had been to school, whether from a bush village or a large

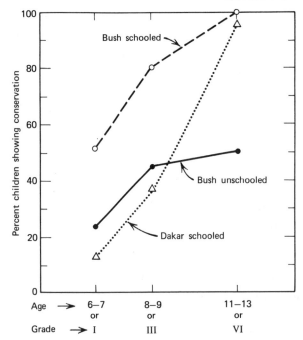

Figure 7-2. Percent of Wolof children of different backgrounds and ages exhibiting conservation of water in two beakers.

city, gave conservation responses. Only half of the nonschool children raised in the bush had achieved conservation by this age. On the basis of these and other findings, Greenfield speculates that in the absence of schooling or school-like experiences "intellectual development, defined as *any* qualitative change, ceases shortly after age nine" (p. 234). When comparison is made with Western norms for the acquisition of conservation in this situation, it is found that the Senegalese children are very similar to Western ones in terms of *grade level*, but because the Senegalese children start school at a later date, they lag slightly behind the Western norms in terms of *age*. The major conclusion from the data presented thus far is that Wolof children who have attended school perform more like Western children than like their nonschooled age mates in the same village.

A good deal of information about the children's understanding of the problem can be obtained from an analysis of the reasons they give for their responses. Greenfield distinguishes three basic kinds of justification: *perceptual* ("they look alike"), *direct-action* (statements about pouring the water from one beaker to the other), and *transformational* ("if you were to pour this one back, it would be the same"). When she examined the relation between conservation and justification, she found that the groups who showed increasing conservation with age showed a parallel decrease in perceptual justification and an increase in the other two kinds of justification. The nonschooled children living in the bush village showed an *increase* in the number of perceptual justifications; it seems that they were fooled by the appearance of the beakers.

One explanation frequently given by the Wolof children in justifying a nonconservation response was to say that the amount of water in the two beakers was no longer the same because the experimenter had poured it. This reason is very rare among Western children. The nature of the justifications given by the Wolof bush children led Greenfield to two modified conservation experiments aimed at exploring the difficulties they experienced.

In the first of these modified experiments, children were first tested with two water beakers in the standard manner to see whether they would manifest conservation. If they did not, a second experiment was carried out. This time the beakers were placed behind a screen with only their tops showing. The child could see the water being poured from one to another, but could not see the water levels in the beakers. One would think that the screening procedure would reduce the child's reliance on perceptual cues and lead to better conservation, but Greenfield found little effect of screening. In fact, perceptual *reasons* were not in the least reduced, even though the stimuli were hidden from sight. This finding contrasted strongly with the results of a similar test administered to American children, who were measurably helped if they had previously failed to conserve and had given a perceptual reason for their choice.

The second experiment was directed at the question of "action magic," the belief of many Wolof children that the experimenter somehow influenced the amount of water present in the two beakers. In this version of the experiment, the nonschooled bush children were allowed to pour for themselves, and conservation increased markedly. This do-it-yourself procedure had no effect at all on nonconserving city schoolchildren who had failed to give action-magic reasons in the first place.

Greenfield's experiments indicate that the conservation task is by no means culture free. She found variations among her different Wolof groups, both on the basic task and in response to manipulations like the action-magic experiment. Thus, even within a single cultural group (the Wolof) performance depends on how the task is presented and the particular past experiences of the subjects (as for instance, whether they live in a rural town or the city, and whether or not they attend school).

While these variations are very clear, the explanation of them is not. Greenfield and Bruner (1969) put forth the view that Wolof children, raised in a traditional setting, never learn to make a distinction between internal (psychological) and external (physical) reality. Wolof child-rearing practices emphasize personal relations and group cohesiveness, not manipulation of objects:

> At the same time as the Wolof child's manipulation of the physical, inanimate world fails to be encouraged in isolation from social relations, the personal desires and intentions which would isolate him from the group are also discouraged. . . . [H]e becomes less and less an individual, more and more a member of a collectivity (pp. 641–642).

As a result of this traditional upbringing, the Wolof child is more likely to give social explanations than physicalistic ones. By contrast, those who are raised in an urban setting, or those who attend school, learn to emphasize explanations based on physical criteria.

This argument bears strong similarities to Berry's notion that ecological demands and socialization practices complement each other to provide coherent constellations of psychological responses to the world. However, as was the case in the studies of the influence of culture on perception, there remain many uncertainties when it comes to explaining why a particular pattern of results has been obtained.

One of the most baffling questions is how we are to interpret the finding that volume conservation is present in only *half* of the 13-year-olds who had no schooling and is, according to Greenfield, absent in nonliterate adults. As Greenfield herself points out, all people have to come to understand certain basic laws of the physical world (or at least behave in accordance with these laws) if they are to survive. Can we imagine an adult who would pour water from a small bucket into a larger one and believe that the amount of water has been decreased by this act? In desert communities where water is a treasured commodity, everyone can be expected to conform to certain laws of conservation.

Since we have already seen that the way people perform on the more traditional concept and classification tasks is very much influenced by the nature of the materials used and the specific problem situations, it seems reasonable to assume that these factors may affect conservation performance also. Will the number of conservers be increased if more familiar test materials are used? One way to approach this problem is to look for cultural situations where children can be expected to have a lot of experience in manipulating a particular physical substance or in dealing with a specific physical problem.

Price-Williams, Gordon, and Ramirez (1969) worked with 76 children, 6 to 9 years old, in the Mexican state of Jalisco, which has many towns famous for their pottery. Half of the children were selected from pottery-making families, the other half from families of a similar socioeconomic status who engaged in other trades.

These investigators hypothesized that practice in pottery making should promote conservation of substance, and that therefore potters' children would perform better on tests of conservation using clay than other children would. This is exactly what they did find. Potters' children also gave more conservation responses in tests for conservation of number, liquid, weight, and volume, but on these the degree of superiority was not statistically reliable.

A second study emphasizing environmentally induced skills was conducted by Dasen (1973) among Aborigines of central Australia. Dasen points out that traditional Aborigines depend on hunting and food gathering for their livelihood. They often travel long distances in their search for food, and in order to survive, they must be able to locate water holes. Although they do not carry maps, they draw maps on the ground to indicate where water holes are located.

On the other hand, Aboriginal languages are very spare in their use of number and measurement terms. Numbers larger than 5 are lumped under a term translated as "big mob." Lack of number and measurement terms is by no means unique to the Aborigine and is usually attributed to the fact that in hunting societies social life is dominated by individuals and very small groups.

This contrast between spatial and measurement demands made by the culture led Dasen to propose that the Aborigine would perform better on spatial tests than on tests involving measurement.

As one of his tests of spatial ability, Dasen used two models of an Australian landscape. The models were placed next to each other, and the child was asked to name the elements of one model while pointing out its mate on the other. Then a toy sheep was placed on one model and the child was asked to place a sheep in the same place on the other model.

Once it was established that the child understood the task, Dasen placed the sheep on one model and rotated the other 180 degrees. The child's task was to place the sheep in the correct place on the rotated model.

Tests of measurement ability included tests for conservation of quantity like those used by Greenfield and tests for conservation of weight, volume, and length.

Three populations of schoolchildren were tested: a group of Aborigines who had not had much contact with Australian-European culture (low-contact group), a medium-contact group, and a group of lower middle-class Australian and European children in Canberra. Small groups of adults from the two Aborigine populations were also given selected tests.

Consistent with his hypothesis, Dasen found that the Aboriginal groups did better on the spatial tests than on the measurement tests. Data from the Canberra children show that this is not simply because the spatial tests are generally easier—the Canberra children performed significantly better on the *measurement* tests than on the spatial tests! This pattern of results fits very nicely with Dasen's hypothesis about the relation between environmental demands, culturally valued skills, and individual cognitive skills.

Dasen obtained two other results that are relevant to the question of which cultural experiences influence the manifestation of conservation under the customary testing procedures. First, he found that the Aborigine group having more contact with Australian-European culture (the medium-contact group) performed consistently better than the low-contact group (a confirmation of an earlier finding among Australian Aborgines by deLacey, 1970). Since the children in both groups were attending school, this suggests that over and above education, or, independently of education, European contact plays an important role in test performance.

Second, many Aborigine schoolchildren 13 to 16 years of age still failed to demonstrate conservation of weight, volume, length, or liquid quantity. What is more, a majority of the adults tested also were nonconservers on these tests, even though Dasen says they tended to represent the younger, better educated, and more acculturated portion of the adult population.

This finding is by no means unique to Dasen. A large number of nonconservers was found among older schoolchildren by de Lemos (1969), who also worked with Australian Aborigines, by deLacey (1970) among New Guinea natives, and by Heron (1971) among Zambians. Clearly, educational experience in European-type schools is not a sufficient explanation for conservation performance, although it appeared to be so from Greenfield's initial studies.

Dasen's summary of Piagetian research (1972) indicates that wherever Piagetian tests have been applied in non-Western cultures (and these have been many, including, in addition to those already mentioned, Iran and China), investigators have found the same stages and sequences in the development of conservation as those originally described by Piaget on the basis of his work with Genevan children. In Dasen's own research (1973) detailed qualitative analysis showed that the reasons given by Aboriginal children for their answers were substantially the same as those given by European children in Canberra, and that their responses and explanations could be classified without difficulty into the stages described by Piaget. This common finding seems to suggest that the conservation performance is the end point of a *course* of development whose sequences are the same from culture to culture. On the other hand, what is referred to as the *rate* of development (measured by the age at which children enter the various stages) has also been consistently found to be slower for non-Western cultures, suggesting a strong influence of cultural and environmental factors. As we have seen, at least three different constellations of such factors have been shown to promote good performance on the kinds of tasks studied intensively by Piaget: the nature of the activities engaged in by members of the culture (or some subgroups, such as potters); involvement in instructional situations such as those provided in a Western-type school; and participation in social interactions with members of a Western culture. These are, of course, rather crude and global identifications of complexes of experiences whose exact nature and differential significance we know very little about. Nor do we know how—*through what mechanisms*—such experiences may contribute to successful performances on Piagetian tasks, and, perhaps more to the point, why they do contribute in some instances and do not in others.

This brings us to the most crucial difficulty we encounter in this area of cross-cultural research: What implications can be drawn from conservation and nonconservation among members of non-Western cultures? Within Piagetian theory, the attainment of various conservation concepts is considered of great developmental significance because these are the indicators that a given child has achieved generalized intellectual structures that make possible a multiplicity of intellectual operations in many different situations and problems. Goodnow and Bethon (1966) found that 11-year-old American children whose conservation performance was superior also showed superior intelligence, as measured by the California Test of Mental Maturity. But for Zambian schoolchildren, Heron (1971) found no relation between conservation of weight and scores on nonverbal reasoning tests from the British Intelligence Scale. The reasoning tests, but not the conservation performance, were related to actual school achievement. Intelligence-test performance and school achievement may well be improper measures for the investigation of the general significance of conservation performance, but we refer to these studies here to emphasize that a relation between conservation performance and other cognitive performance obtained in our culture does not hold in another. Until some relation between conservation performance and other cognitive skills is demonstrated in non-Western cultures, it is difficult to arrive at any judgment of its significance.

This is especially true in light of the difficulty of coming to grips with what nonconservation might mean. In Europe and the United States, where all normal children eventually come to respond correctly across the whole spectrum of conservation problems, such a statement as "55 to 60 percent of the 5- to 6-year-olds conserve" has a relatively clear interpretation—55 to 60 percent of the children have entered the concrete-operational stage that *all* children *eventually* enter; the culture is homogenous with respect to adult performance. But the various traditional societies we have been studying are *not* homogenous with respect to their level of cognitive maturity as measured by conservation performance: some adults conserve, some do not.

What does it mean to claim that "tribe X does not mature past the European 11-year stage" if 50 percent of the members of tribe X conserve and 50 percent do not? No one in tribe X is operating at the "11-year-old-level" and to speak of a "leveling off of cognitive development" as if the statement applies to individuals is a serious mistake. Until we have some better idea of what induces some members of traditional societies to solve conservation problems while their neighbors do not, we cannot be certain about the significance of conservation tests as a tool for understanding the relation between culture and cognitive development.

Inferential Combination

Thinking is conceived of by some psychologists as a process by which familiar elements are combined in a new way to reach a goal. This concept is clearly embodied in an experiment first developed for the study of reasoning in rats (Maier, 1929) and applied to children by Kendler and Kendler (1967). The apparatus used in this research is shown in Figure 7–3.

It consists of a metal box, divided into three panels (A, B, and C) each with its own door. The subject is first taught that he can get a *marble* by pushing the button in the middle of Panel A. During this training, the doors to Panels B and C remain closed. In the next step, the doors to Panels A and B remain closed and the subject is taught that he can get a *ball bearing* by pushing the button in Panel C. Next, with Panels A and C closed, he is taught that he can obtain a piece of candy by putting a marble in Box B. Finally, all three panel doors are opened simultaneously for the first time, and the subject is told to do whatever is necessary to get the candy.

Formally, this problem represents the requirements for a study of thinking outlined above. The subject has to combine two independently learned acts in a new combination (open Box A

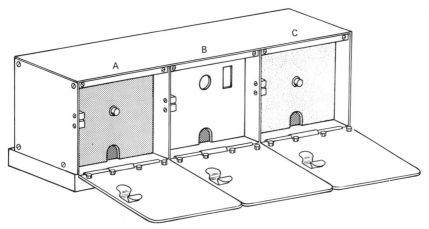

Figure 7-3. Apparatus used to study inference (after illustration in Cole, Gay, Glick, and Sharp, 1971).

to get the marble; take the marble and put it in Box B to get the candy) in order to attain his goal.

As simple as the problem appears, it is absolutely beyond the capacity of rats. Even children up to the age of about 10 years are likely to experience difficulty with it.

When this experiment was first tried out in Liberia among tribal people of various ages, they all experienced difficulty (Cole et al., 1971). Only 8 percent of the traditional, nonliterate Kpelle adults spontaneously pushed the button that yielded the marble and then placed the marble in the hole in the center panel, which yielded the candy. There were no differences among the traditional subjects as a function of age: 5- and 6-year-olds performed about as well as young adults. This percentage of correct inferential responses corresponds roughly with the performance obtained with American kindergartners (Kendler, Kendler, and Carrick, 1966).

The situation is only slightly improved by education. Groups of 9- to 12-year-old and 17- to 20-year-old students averaged 25 to 30 percent spontaneously correct inferential responses. But American third-graders obtained a score of 53 percent correct. We might be tempted to conclude at this point that the noneducated Kpelle finds it difficult to make simple inferences and that although schooling helps a little, it does not help much.

Before jumping to any such conclusions, a fuller characterization of the behavior of our subjects as well as some more experimentation are both in order. For one thing, we noted that many of the subjects seemed genuinely frightened of the apparatus. Many spent inordinate amounts of time playing with screws that held the apparatus together, sticking their fingers into the hole from which the candy emerged, and generally indulging in a lot of extraneous behavior. Very often, if the experimenter prompted the subject by asking, "Which button should you press so that you can get the candy?" the subject would press both buttons simultaneously. In short, it was not clear that the subjects understood either the instructions or how to use the strange apparatus.

The next stage of experimentation was an effort to come up with a Kpelle version of the same problem—that is, a problem that had the same logical structure, but made use of materials familiar to all Kpelle people.

The solution was to use a locked box containing a piece of candy as the goal object. The box could be opened with a key (keys and locks are now generally available in central Liberia). At the start of the experiment, two keys were shown to the subject, one painted red, the other black. The keys were then placed in two identifiably different matchboxes. In the first phase of the experiment, the subject learned which matchbox contained which key (this is analogous to learning which panel contains the marble in the original version). Then the matchboxes were set aside, the two keys were presented, and the subject learned which key fit the lock and made it possible to obtain the candy. (This is analogous to learning that the marble and not the ball bearing produced the candy when inserted in the center panel of the original apparatus.) Finally, the subject was presented with the two matchboxes and the locked box and told to do whatever was necessary to get the candy.

The change in response to the problem was dramatic when the key-lock procedure was introduced. From 70 to 80 percent of the subjects (aged 7 through adulthood) solved the problem spontaneously and 90 percent solved it with a little prompting. This way of conducting the experiment makes it look as if the Kpelle experience no difficulty at all with a simple inferential problem—provided that they are familiar with its elements.

It is possible, however, that in choosing a new form for the problem, we were doing more than simply changing the particular elements. Consider the second form of the problem again. Putting keys in locks is almost certainly a very well learned response for subjects who know about keys and locks. In fact, a key might be defined as something that opens a lock. If this is the case, we may have inadvertently been providing our Kpelle subjects with half of the answer to their problem in the key-lock version, thus making them look more competent than they would look if they had to learn the whole problem in the situation itself.

These ambiguities led to still another experiment, this time aimed at determining whether a previously learned link between the goal and the object used to obtain the goal made it easier to solve this kind of inference problem.

In this second experiment both Kpelle and American children were studied. The two conditions of greatest interest involved combinations of the procedures (and apparatus) used in the first two experiments. In the first of these conditions, subjects obtained a red or black key from Panels A or C of the apparatus pictured in Figure 7–3; one of these keys could be used to unlock the box from the second experiment. In the other condition the subjects obtained keys from matchboxes, one of which caused a candy to drop when it was placed in panel B of the original apparatus. The results were completely contrary to our expectations: performance was best when the keys were taken from matchboxes and dropped into the center panel of the original apparatus. Performance when keys were obtained from that apparatus and then used to open the locked box was no better than performance in the original experiment.

From this new experiment we can conclude that the difficulty that young children and tribal Liberians experience with our simple inference task is that they do not know how to begin. For some reason, the process involved in obtaining a marble or a key from the side panel of the original apparatus interferes with later phases of the response sequence. Cultural differences seem in this case to reside in the kinds of initial situations that promote a good beginning for problem solution, not in the ability to link separately learned elements in order to solve a problem.

This experimental sequence illustrates the care that has to be taken before a conclusion about cultural differences can be firmly grounded. In the process of tracking down the source of the difference between cultural groups, we not only located the point at which the determining differences occur, but extended our knowledge of one small aspect of problem-solving behavior as well. Even such a small step forward required a good deal of work, perhaps more than the particular example of inferential behavior warranted. But progress in understanding the relation between cultural variables and such cognitive processes as inferential reasoning is probably only to be achieved by the accumulation of such little steps; jumping straight to a successful design may leave us uncertain of where we have landed.

Verbal Logical Problems

Not all studies of reasoning and problem solving have to involve pouring water and opening boxes, although psychologists tend to rely heavily on such activities in their investigations. It is also possible to study reasoning by purely verbal means, although, as we shall see, the pitfalls in such an undertaking are legion.

It has been established in several American-based studies of logical reasoning that when presented a formal logical problem, subjects are often fooled by the content of the problem into drawing conclusions that do not follow from the premises. For example, we are all familiar with the following problem:

All men are mortal.
Socrates is a man.
∴. Socrates is mortal.

We would all accept this conclusion as following from the premises, and if presented the premises alone, we could most likely arrive at the proper conclusion.

But what about the following problem?

All communists say that they seek nothing but peace.
The longshoremen's union says that it seeks nothing but peace.
∴. The longshoremen are communists.

In this case the conclusion does *not* follow from the premises, but anyone who reads the daily newspapers can find many instances of such reasoning in the comments of officials and common citizens alike.

Research into the processes underlying nonlogical responses to such verbal logical problems has not proceeded much past the observation that content often determines acceptability of the conclusions, independent of the structure of the problem. However, what few cross-cultural data exist indicate that even the seemingly simple matter of responding to such a problem in its own terms is a learned convention.

The earliest data on this problem were collected by Soviet psychologists who were students of L. S. Vygotsky, and most notably by A. R. Luria, in the early 1930s (Luria, 1971). He presented two kinds of verbal syllogisms to collectivized and non-collectivized central Asian peasants: the contents of some were taken from the concrete, practical experience of the villagers; the contents of others bore no relation to familiar, practical life. An example of a practical problem was the following: "Cotton grows where it is hot and humid. In the village it is hot and humid. Does cotton grow there or not?" For syllogisms not connected with practical experience, he gave such logical problems as, "In the north, where there is snow all year, the bears are white. Town X is in the north. Are the bears white in that town or not?" Handling the first type of problem presented no difficulty to the subjects. They would draw the correct conclusion, but would characteristically support their answers by appealing to the facts of experience: "And that's the way it is; I know myself."

The second kind of syllogism was responded to quite differently. A typical response to the white bear problem was the answer: "How should I know what color the bear was? It was your friend that saw him, ask your friend." Almost all of the uncollectivized, nonschooled peasants replied to the problems in a similar way— they refused to accept the system of logical assumptions and to draw conclusions from them. On the other hand, people from the same villages who had had a small amount of schooling or who were engaged in collective planning of farm production accepted the problems on their own terms and drew correct conclusions.

Research among Kpelle tribesmen in Liberia indicates that their responses are like those of the central Asian peasant. The problems that were presented differed from the traditional syllogisms used by Luria; nevertheless, they called for various forms of logical inference, and the materials were culturally familiar. The following interview selections give the quality of the great majority of responses. The experimenter is a local Kpelle man, the speakers are esteemed village elders.

Example 1

> *Experimenter:* At one time spider went to a feast. He was told to answer this question before he could eat any of the food. The question is: Spider and black deer always eat together. Spider is eating. Is black deer eating?
>
> *Subject:* Were they in the bush?
>
> *Experimenter:* Yes.
>
> *Subject:* Were they eating together?
>
> *Experimenter:* Spider and black deer always eat together. Spider is eating. Is black deer eating?
>
> *Subject:* But I was not there. How can I answer such a question?
>
> *Experimenter:* Can't you answer it? Even if you were not there, you can answer it. (Repeats the question.)
>
> *Subject:* Oh, oh, black deer is eating.
>
> *Experimenter:* What is your reason for saying that black deer was eating?
>
> *Subject:* The reason is that black deer always walks about all day eating green leaves in the bush. Then he rests for a while and gets up again to eat.

Like the central Asian peasant, this Kpelle tribal leader attempts to handle the problem on a *factual* basis. Mary Henle (1962), who has made extensive studies of syllogistic reasoning and whose analysis of sources of error is drawn upon here, characterizes this mode of response as a "failure to accept the logical task." The subject's failure to grasp the general concept of logical validity is illustrated by his query as to how he might be expected to answer the question when "he wasn't there." His effort to find a factual basis for arriving at a conclusion is indicated by his questions eliciting additional facts ("were they in the bush?" "were they eating together?"). When the experimenter is uncooperative, the subject finally "produces" some facts to support an answer. There is clearly involved here a process of active reasoning—but one proceeding from evidence that is real and experiential, rather than from the theoretical evidence incorporated in the problem.

Other transformations typically introduced into the problem to permit its "solution" on a factual basis are displayed in the following transcript:

Example 2

> *Experimenter:* If Flumo or Yakpalo drinks cane juice, the Town Chief gets vexed. Flumo is not drinking cane juice. Yakpalo is drinking cane juice. Is the Town Chief vexed?
>
> *Subject:* People do not get vexed with two persons.
>
> *Experimenter:* (Repeats the problem.)
>
> *Subject:* The Town Chief was not vexed on that day.
>
> *Experimenter:* The Town Chief was not vexed? What is the reason?
>
> *Subject:* The reason is that he doesn't love Flumo.
>
> *Experimenter:* He doesn't love Flumo? Go on with the reason.
>
> *Subject:* The reason is that Flumo's drinking is a hard time. That is why when he drinks cane juice, the Town Chief gets vexed. But sometimes when Yakpalo drinks cane juice, he will not give a hard time to people. He goes to lie down to sleep. At that rate people do not get vexed with him. But people who drink and go about fighting—the Town Chief cannot love them in the town.

It appears that this subject had a set of particular characters in mind (a certain Flumo with whom he was acquainted, perhaps) and was concerned with arriving at a conclusion that expressed the social truth as he knew it. To effect this end, he rejected the first premise of the problem and substituted for it another statement (people do not get vexed with two people). Then, like our first subject, he imported new evidence into the problm (facts about Flumo's and Yakpalo's behavior when drunk, for example), which permitted a conclusion *both* logically valid *and* factually true. While this subject's answer is "wrong" as far as the experimental problem is concerned, it is the outcome of a beautiful piece of logical reasoning from new premises. We can easily see this by recasting his statements into more traditional syllogistic form:

> Flumo's drinking gives people a hard time. (Explicit premise)
> Yakpalo's drinking does not give people a hard time. (Explcit premise)
> People do not get vexed when they are not given a hard time. (Explicit premise)
> The Town Chief is a person. (Implicit premise)
> Therefore, the Town Chief is not vexed at Yakpalo. (Conclusion)

These examples are representative of findings in a study involving a large number of subjects and different kinds of logical problems (Cole et al., 1971, Chap. 6). Overall, only 33 percent of the problems were answered correctly, and a great majority of the correct responses were for the wrong reason. In a follow-up study, responses of traditional adults were compared with those of a group of young adult high school students: 90 percent of student responses were correct, and their answers were very much in the Western mold. Next, groups of 10- to 14-year-old children with varying degrees of schooling were studied. The children who had never attended school responded like the traditional adults; children who had reached the third grade responded more like the high-schoolers. Hence it appears that some experiences involved in Western-style education change the "set" taken to these problems so that the logical relations that they express, rather than their factual content, constrain the conclusions reached.

Up to this point, we have the beginnings of a descriptive account of how traditional people handle verbal logical problems. But we are not even this far advanced in understanding *why* logical relations seldom govern subjects' conclusions. Do the relations among verbal propositions constitute a specific source of difficulty? Or is it the case that the subject processes the relational information but chooses to ignore it when it conflicts with his personal experience?

In an effort to get at some of these problems, Scribner (1973b) followed up on an observation of Luria's. Luria had observed that when subjects tried to repeat a question, they frequently dropped the relational terms and rendered the major and minor premises as two isolated statements. Scribner somewhat modified the procedure to incorporate a requirement that the subject recall the problem at two points in the experiment. First, the subject answered the problem, stated his reason, and was asked to recall the problem; then the experimenter slowly reread the problem and the subject was asked to recall it immediately. If the subject omitted the question at the end of the problem in either of his recall attempts, the experimenter prompted him by inquiring, "What question did I ask you?" The first recall, given after the subject had wrestled with the problem and come up with an answer, was often fragmentary and contained transformations of the kind already discussed. But a striking and unexpected finding was that the second recall, given immediately after the subject reheard the problem, was often no more complete nor accurate than the first! A second prominent feature of the recalls was that the question contained in the problem was frequently stated as a conclusion— a statement of fact. Here are a few examples:

Example 1

    Problem: The chief's brother either gave him a goat or he gave him a chicken.
    The chief's brother did not give him a goat. Did he give him a chicken?

    Subject's answer and reason: Yes. I know he gave it to him.

    Subject's first recall: The chief's brother will give him a goat. If he does not give him a goat, he will give him a chicken.

    Experimenter: What question did I ask?

    Subject: You asked me, is the chief's brother going to give him a goat?

    Experimenter: (Reads the problem again.)

    Subject's second recall: Yes. That is what you told me. The chief's brother will give him a goat. If he does not give him a goat, he will give him a chicken.

    Experimenter: What question did I ask you?

    Subject: You asked me, the chief's brother will give him a goat. If he does not give him a goat, will he give him a chicken?

If we inspect this protocol carefully, we will observe that at no time during the entire procedure does the subject reproduce all the information that is necessary to reach a conclusion; the information that the brother did not give the chief a goat has dropped out entirely. The several attempts to recall the problem, moreover, indicate that without this information, the subject had difficulty keeping the problem question in mind—again, necessary information for the correct solution. Lacking evidence, our respondent solved his special problem of acquitting himself in the experimental task by giving an essentially arbitrary answer: *"I know* he gave it to him."

Example 2

    Problem: Some kwi (Western) people are wealthy.
    All wealthy people are powerful. Are some kwi people powerful?

    Subject's answer and reason: Yes. It is because some kwi are wealthy and they have power.

    Subject's first recall: Some kwi in this town are wealthy. They have power.

Experimenter: What question did I ask you?
Subject: Do some kwi have power?
Experimenter: (Reads the problem again.)
Subject's second recall: Some kwi are wealthy. They have power. Do many wealthy men have power?

In this example we observe the disappearance of the generalizing proposition, "All wealthy people are powerful," which is an essential condition for a correct conclusion and the transformation of the question into a piece of evidence. To the extent that the subject's reproduction of the problem accurately represents the one he was in fact attempting to solve (and for many reasons, which we will not take up here, we cannot be entirely sure of this), the examples we have quoted seem to be instances in which subjects were disposing of the experimental task by giving essentially arbitrary answers or by answering on the basis of general knowledge (in Liberia, kwi people *are* both wealthy and powerful). These were perhaps sensible ways of handling the task, but they represent a different mode of problem solution from the examples of creative constructions of appropriate (factually congruent) problems we encountered in the first interviews.

The techniques we have relied on to help us get at the actual thinking processes of the subjects, and away from inferences based entirely on the correctness or incorrectness of answers, are still new and in need of refinement and testing before they can give us reliable information. They have been useful, however, in helping us reformulate the questions with which we are dealing. It is quite clear that we cannot draw conclusions about reasoning processes from the *answers* people give to logic problems. We have first to ask: "What is their understanding of the task? How do they encode the information presented to them? What transformations does the information undergo, and what factors control these?

Before going on to conclude something about the ability of nonliterate peoples to reason verbally, a different form of reasoning problem must be described. In this study conducted by John Gay (1971) the material was presented in a familiar folk-tale context. The problem involved a judgment based on a comparison of relations between elements expressed in the form of verbal logical connectives (*and, or, if . . . then*). The story in one of its forms is as follows:

> This is an old matter. You must listen carefully and think about the answer, so that you can answer the questions in a sensible way.
>
> Two men named Flumo and Yakpalo were wanting to marry, and so they went on the road to find beautiful girls. They came to a man's house and found that the man had a beautiful daughter. Each one brought gifts for the marriage. The gifts were money and sickness. They told the man, "if you do not marry your daughter to one of us and take the gifts he offers, we will kill you."
>
> Flumo said, "You must take money *and* sickness."
>
> Yakpalo said, "You must take money *or* sickness."
>
> Which one did the man give his daughter to and why?

In other forms of the story there were systematic variations in the gifts offered and in the logical connectives used between the gifts in each man's statement. In some cases both gifts were good, in some only one was good, and in some both were bad. The person interviewed was required to choose the most advantageous or least harmful combination of gifts. Each subject was scored as to whether his answer was correct, incorrect, or irrelevant; an example of an irrelevant answer was that the respondent would rather die than accept either suitor, if both offered bad gifts.

Gay presented the problems to three groups of Kpelle subjects, two of them nonliterate (one of 18- to 25-year-olds, the other of 40- to 50-year-olds) and the third consisting of 18- to 25-year-old high school students. In addition, 36 American college students were given the same set of problems. The most interesting result of this study is that the American college students and all the Kpelle groups had the same percentage of wrong answers—there were no group differences in errors. But the American college students exceeded all three Kpelle groups in the percentage of *correct* answers. This seeming paradox is accounted for by the fact that fully one-fifth of the Kpelle replies (in each of the experimental groups) was irrelevant. And irrelevant answers were given almost exclusively when a decision had to be made between two bad choices; under these circumstances, the Kpelle tended to avoid the issue, while the Americans sought to make the best of a bad bargain. It would appear that the Kpelle subjects were as able to avoid errors as the American college students, but they were much more likely to deviate from the solution pattern set up by the experimenter in order to give a more socially appropriate response.

What can we conclude from this series of studies? For one thing, with all the varied materials and procedures that have been used, we have encountered no examples of thinking that violate the logical law of contradiction. On the contrary, our preliminary analysis shows that the major sources of error in Kpelle performance are of the same kinds as those involved in the reasoning of American college students (Henle, 1962). What we have encountered among people in traditional societies is a refusal to remain within the boundaries of the problem presented by the experimenter. In the case of the more standard experimental material (syllogistic reasoning), the terms of the problem were often not accepted or were modified; additional information was supplied in order to bring the statements and their implications into closer conformity with the factual world of experience. In the folk-tale problem, subjects tended to reject the restricted set of possible solutions if the outcome violated some standard of social truth. We know, too, that when traditional people have some schooling (as in our studies in Liberia) or become involved in complex acts of social planning (Luria's data), verbal problems of this kind are accepted, and reasoning is constrained by the structure of the problem. Why this switchover occurs is a challenging problem for investigation. And equally challenging is the task of adapting traditional procedures so that they yield a detailed account of how, in fact, traditional people do reason when they are presented with hypothetical verbal problems.

Summary

A real irony is embodied in this chapter. For more than a hundred years, speculation about the relation between culture and cognition has centered on the issues we have just been reviewing. Yet so few psychological studies of problem solving in differing cultural settings have been conducted that a summary of this work can have little content.

We can identify three reasons for the discontinuity between interest and accomplishment. First, as we attempted to make clear in the opening pages of this chapter, there is an important sense in which psychologists and other social scientists are not talking about the same topic when they refer to culture, logic, and problem solving. There is no way to test Levy-Bruhl's assertions about primitive mind by referring to the amount of water in two glasses. He explicitly excluded such activities from consideration. Yet psychology has developed no generally agreed upon techniques for studying the cognitive mechanisms at work in the domain of beliefs.

Second, with the exception of the Piagetian research (which we have only sampled here), there really is no solid body of research on culture and problem solving using techniques and problems that psychologists view as legitimate. One reason for this is the paucity of problem-solving research anywhere in psychology in the last thirty years. There are a variety of interesting problem-solving situations that could be studied to good purpose in cross-cultural contexts, however, and some techniques are available for tackling them. For example, one of the few statements to grow out of Levi-Strauss' work that could be readily studied by psychologists is his characterization of the primitive problem solver as a *bricoleur* (see Chapter 2, pp. 26–27). A *bricoleur* is a jack-of-all-trades, a man who makes flexible use of his instruments, a man who does not fixate on a single attribute of objects and so can use them in a variety of ways. This suggests that primitive people should be less subject to *functional fixedness* (the inability to use an object in a nonstandard way to solve a novel problem) than are those in more technologically developed societies. No studies have followed up this hypothesis.

At the moment, the greatest source of suggestions for problem-solving studies is the anthropological literature, although psychologists will have to turn such work to their own uses. For example, Gladwin (1969) provides fascinating examples of complex navigation skills developed by nonliterate sailing people in the South Pacific.

In his well-known work on Yacqui Indian sorcery, Carlos Castenada gives many examples of Don Juan's thinking that seem reminiscent of Levy-Bruhl's descriptions of "primitive mentality." At the same time, Don Juan is presented as a man who, in his interpersonal relations, demonstrates problem-solving techniques compelling enough to greatly influence Castenada himself (1968).

Bringing such observations together with psychological research is a giant order, and an issue that we will take up explicitly in the next chapter.

We would speculate that the third reason for the paucity of problem-solving research is that studies on this topic are so difficult to interpret, even within familiar cultural contexts. The key here is that problem solving, in ways that are pervasive and compelling, is always seen as a component of a larger behavioral network in which perception, memory, classification, and all other cognitive processes play a role. It is virtually impossible to isolate problem solving as a "thing."

Here cross-cultural research seems to be in a position to make some modest contribution to theories about the development of thinking. In a dramatic way, it highlights the need to analyze *all* the components involved in problem-solving tasks before inferences are made about reasoning processes or logical structures *per se.* Secondly, cross-cultural research might make a contribution to the development of a general theory of thinking. There are indications that a number of specific experiential factors play important roles in performance on classical psychological problem-solving tasks: familiarity with materials, opportunities presented by the environment for exploring spatial relationships, social contact with urbanized people, attendance at Western-type schools—all have been implicated as factors in the performance of one or more tasks. Yet there is no theory of thinking that seems at the present time to handle these varied constellations of experience within a single coherent framework.

But what can we say about problem solving among traditional people? The most firmly based, and perhaps the most important, conclusion we can reach at the present time is that thus far there is no evidence for different *kinds* of reasoning processes such as the old classic theories alleged—we have no evidence for a "primitive" logic. To go beyond this to a positive characterization of *how* traditional people think will require a host of new techniques and a great deal of imaginative thinking on the part of psychologists.

chapter 8 *Culture and Cognition: trees in search of a forest*

In the preceding pages we have reviewed a large number of studies whose subjects and subject matters have ranged across the globe and across a broad spectrum of the problems involved in the study of the role of culture in cognition. In looking back over the material covered, one cannot avoid the feeling that somewhere along the line important questions have been sidetracked. Our somewhat cautious and circumspect introduction is now easier to understand—the accomplishments of psychologists seeking to understand the relation between culture and cognition have been modest indeed. We can now plainly see that phrases such as "the mind of the primitive" have no clear referents in the real world and generate questions that have no answers, such as: "Does the mind of the primitive differ from the mind of technological man?" But the questions that have been posed in place of these general and unresolvable phrases seem to be not nearly as significant: the question of whether or not education influences concept formation gets translated into studies of whether or not children make particular kinds of judgments about the consequences of pouring water from one glass to another.

This sequence, from grand speculation to narrowly specified experimental conditions is not, of course, restricted to cross-cultural psychological research. But we have been dealing with an area of human knowledge that has evoked enormously broad speculation; the gap between the kinds of statements we would like to make and the statements actually warranted by empirical evidence is very wide indeed.

The key problem, as we have been emphasizing throughout this book, is that any fact, or small set of facts, is open to a wide variety of interpretations. So long as we are only concerned with demonstrating that human cultural groups differ enormously in their beliefs and theories about the world and in their art products and technological accomplishments, there can be no question: there are marked and multitudinous cultural differences. But are these differences the result of differences in basic *cognitive processes*, or are they merely the expressions of the many products that a universal human mind can manufacture, given wide variations in conditions of life and culturally valued activities?

Our review has not answered this question. But it has suggested that obstacles to asking (and beginning to answer) this and other central questions about culture and cognition arise from weaknesses in both theory and empirical investigation. Such a conclusion might seem fatuous; yet only because attempts have been made to put theories to the test have the ambiguities and weaknesses of global, undifferentiated concepts about Mind and Man become apparent. Conversely, efforts to pull together and interpret facts accumulated from a variety of disconnected experiments have succeeded in revealing the lack of an integrating theory, without which unambiguous interpretation is impossible. What we have learned from the pioneer thinkers and investigators in the field is a long list of how-not-to's—how not to ask questions, and how not to go about investigating them. We also have a shorter, more tentative list of how-to's. We will try to summarize some of these observations and their implications in this chapter. If at times our emphasis seems one-sidedly negative, our justification is that in the long run it will be more productive to direct our criticism at the deficiencies of our science rather than at the alleged deficiencies of the people we study.

To begin with, we have seen more than ample evidence of how *not* to ask questions about culture and cognition. If we were to restrict ourselves to the many studies that have been conducted because the experimenter wanted to "see what the X's would do when presented this task" (IQ test, visual illusion, conservation problem), no reasonable specification of the relation between culture and cognitive processes would be forthcoming. There is simply no way to evaluate the sources of variation when aborigines do not respond to an IQ test in the same way Cambridge undergraduates do. This seemingly simple fact is widely acknowledged and just as widely ignored.

But even when we turn to more sophisticated research—studies involving variations in instructions, motivational conditions, and populations—we find serious problems of conception and interpretation. Among the problems we have emphasized, the following are most pervasive:

1. There is a great readiness to assume that particular kinds of tests or experimental situations are diagnostic of particular cognitive capacities or processes.

2. Psychological processes are treated as "entities," which a person "has" or "does not have" as a property of the person independent of the problem situation. They are also considered to operate independently of each other.

3. Closely related to (1) and (2) is a readiness to believe that poor performance on a particular test is reflective of a deficiency in, or lack of, "the" process that the test is said to measure.

4. Evidence from other disciplines (especially anthropology and linguistics) is usually not taken into account in making inferences about the cognitive processes which a given cultural group has or uses.

5. The complexity of the cultural groups and institutions studied is very often grossly oversimplified.

It will be helpful to keep these general lines of criticism in mind in the discussion that follows, because they represent a kind of catalogue of negative virtues that we believe the psychological study of culture and cognition should not have. By implication, they suggest an approach to future research. These criticisms raise questions about basic concepts and research strategies applicable to the entire field of psychology as well as about those unique to cross-cultural endeavors, but we will deal with them only in the latter context. In developing these criticisms, we will begin where we initially began—with points of view about cognition and how it can be tested. We will then, by way of illustration, present a particular theoretical problem, assess the limitations of the evidence brought to bear on it to date, and outline what we see as the necessary ingredients of a research program to resolve some of the issues involved. Finally, we will double back to the original question animating this entire area of research: Are there *really* cognitive differences among different peoples, or are observed differences in behavior and belief merely varied expressions of a universal human mind?

Are Tests "Diagnostic" of Cognitive Capacities?

As we have seen, many cross-cultural studies set out to determine whether or not some particular group described by anthropologists "has," or "has more," or "has less," of some cognitive capacity considered characteristic of normal psychological functioning in industrialized Western societies. Do rural Africans have *3-D perception* of pictorial material? Do they show *abstract thought?* Have they complex processes of *perceptual analysis?* The *logical structure* of conservation? Questions of this kind imply that each of these terms designates some psychological entity, which is the property of a person and which is measurable by a specifiable—and limited—set of operations. With these assumptions in mind and a measuring instrument (test or experimental paradigm) in hand, the psychologist journeys forth to explore the relation between culture and Entity X. To make the dilemmas he encounters more concrete, let us first simplify the case and consider the problems a cross-cultural investigator would have if he wanted to explain the effect of culture on some nonpsychological characteristic—body temperature, for example. He would, of course, be careful to select people who were suffering no known illness, and he could include, as variables for study, the age of the people, the social structure that characterizes their society, their language, and a host of other factors. Although it is counterfactual, imagine for a moment that he found group differences in temperature. He would then face the problem of *explaining* the source of these differences. He would, of course, want to check the hypothesis that what he was observing were not cultural differences, but physiological differences (much as Berry, 1971, was led to reassess a cultural interpretation of susceptibility to the Muller-Lyer illusion in terms of skin pigmentation). He might also want to check for the possibility that physical factors (altitude, rainfall) are associated with cultural variations, so that he could rule out the possibility that some factor like altitude is responsible for the observed group differences (a not-impossible factor—several anthropologists have sought explanations for cultural differences in variations in the physical ecology).

In short, he will face all of the problems that the psychologist faces when he moves from the documentation of group differences to the explanation of them.

But as a culture–temperature theorist, he will not face a central problem that the psychologist does face. He might have to be cautious about the influence of extremely high altitudes on temperature measurement, but at least he knows that thermometers *measure temperature.*

We do not have analogous information about psychological tests. In a very important sense, we do not know what they measure. Consider the best known of all psychological tests, the IQ test. So long as IQ tests are treated *solely* in terms of their ability to predict a child's school performance, arguments about the nature of the test need not arise. But as soon as we ask, What do IQ tests *really* measure? we enter an area of seemingly endless arguments and ambiguity; there are almost as many definitions of what intelligence *really* is as there are psychologists giving tests. And note that these problems arise before we get to the question: What determines the "amount" of intelligence in a particular child or cultural group? The problems arise, of course, because intelligence is not a property of individuals in the same sense that temperature is. To treat intelligence as if it could be measured like temperature leads us into a variety of absurdities, not the least of which is that we treat an intelligence test like a thermometer.

Similar remarks apply to virtually all psychological tests when they are treated as instruments measuring a fixed capacity. Research on memory conducted prior to 1906 gave us procedures for the study of memory that are still widely used today. These procedures embody our commonsense notion that if we can recall at a later time some material we previously had learned, we can

be said to have "remembered" it. But does the Ebbinghaus procedure (or any other) measure our *memory*? Is memory for
nonsense syllables the same as memory for childhood events or
memory for popular songs? Put this way, it becomes clear that we
cannot treat psychological functions as if they are unitary entities
to which we can apply a "thermometer."

All of this simply argues for taking seriously the notion that in
cognition, as in other areas of psychological functioning, we are
dealing with processes, not with properties. We gain understanding of cultural variations in memory or thinking or concept formation when we can specify the operations that go to make
them up in given situations and how these operations and situations differ from one population to another. In the cross-cultural context, this means that we want to ask questions about how
a particular group goes about interpreting pictorial material,
learning a discrimination problem, classifying geometric stimuli,
and the like.

We know, too, that in almost every area of research reviewed
in this book, the nature of the operations subjects use has been
shown to be sensitive to a whole host of factors connected with
the particular problem situation: the specific demands of the task
(giving a verbal description of a picture, selecting a match, or
"modeling" it), the task material (whether it is familiar or
strange, represented by objects or pictures), the semantic content of the problem (factually true or factually false syllogisms),
the response mode (adjusting a rod in a frame or finding a hidden
picture). Because little attention has been paid to them, we have
altogether neglected motivational, attitudinal, and other factors
that also may affect how the person goes about the experimental
task. Again these considerations argue against the practice of
treating tests or experiments that deal with performance in some
common area (verbal recall, for example) as though, in fact, they
are all getting at the *same thing*.

Finally, if we agree that we are studying operations, not
entities, and that these operations are "shifty" and may work
differently in different circumstances, then it follows that experiments are unlikely to allow us to rank different people in terms
of the "existence" or "amount" of any particular cognitive process. Since this point is central to all cross-cultural research, we
will illustrate how this approach to what cognition is and what
experiments measure can help us thread our way through the

paradoxes encountered in testing a particular hypothesis about cultural effects on cognition.

A Cross-Cultural Hypothesis

For this purpose, we shall pick a problem that has not been dealt with in the previous chapters.

A number of anthropologists writing about the learning processes of nonliterate peoples have remarked on the fact that learning and teaching are almost always an integral part of ongoing activity such as hunting or a round of household chores (Fortes, 1938; Mead, 1964). Children are said to learn by observing.

Observational learning is usually contrasted with learning that is acquired primarily through the medium of language. Mead points out, for example, that in traditional societies adults rarely formulate a particular practice in words or rules; instead, they demonstrate what is to be done. Fortes observes that traditional children (he worked with the Tale people of Ghana) were rarely heard to ask *why* questions. He concludes that such questions are rare because so much of the child's learning occurs in real-life situations where the meaning is intrinsic to the context.

If these anthropological observations and speculations are correct, we might hypothesize two cognitive consequences of a reliance on learning by observation. First, we might expect to find that people who have a lot of practice in learning by observation will be good at it—they will learn quickly if given the chance to learn by observing. Second, these same people ought to experience special difficulties if they are asked to teach or learn something when the teacher and student are not engaged in a common, ongoing activity.

Our next problem is to turn these speculations into observations that are appropriate for experimental, psychological analysis.

Is there an experimental situation that has been developed to tap learning and teaching skills when learner and teacher do not have a shared, meaningful context for carrying out their tasks? There is. It is referred to in the research literature as the "communication experiment." Let us turn to a description of it as it was used by Cole, Gay, and Glick (1969) to study learning and teaching skills among the Kpelle.

A Communication Experiment

The example we have chosen to discuss involves an experimental situation appropriate to testing learning and teaching skills out of context.

Two men are seated at a table. The men are Kpelle rice farmers from central Liberia. Every year since they were small boys they have gone into the jungle to clear patches of land where up-land rice is grown. They know the forest and its vegetation well; they work there almost every day; it gives them food, building materials, tools, and medicines.

On the table in front of them are 10 pairs of sticks (pieces of wood of different kinds) divided into two piles, each pile having one member of every pair. One pile is in front of each man.

A barrier is then placed between the men so that they can neither see each other nor each other's sticks. The experimenter, who is sitting where both men can see him, picks a stick from the speaker's pile and lays it on the table at the speaker's left. The speaker is told to describe the stick so that his partner (the listener) can pick its mate out of his pile.

After hearing the description, the listener tries to select the appropriate stick from his pile. The experimenter then picks out a second stick, places it next to the first stick on the speaker's side, and asks the speaker to describe it so the listener can find the mate in his pile and put it in place. This procedure is continued until all 10 sticks have been described by the speaker and laid out in a row in front of him, and the listener has tried to duplicate these activities.

At this point, the barrier is lifted, and the men are asked to compare the two rows of sticks to see whether they have correctly matched pairs. Errors are described and discussed, and the whole process is then repeated for a second trial.

Descriptions of a set of sticks as we might give them and as they were given by a Kpelle speaker on two trials of an experiment session are listed in Table 8–1.

What is striking about this man's performance (and it is representative of the performance of the many traditional Kpelle rice farmers who participated in this study) is that he is failing to include in his description features that must be communicated if the message is to be received unambigously.

Table 8-1.

English Description	Kpelle Description (First Trial)	Kpelle Description[a] (Second Trial)
thickest straight wood	one of the sticks	one of the sticks
medium straight wood	not a large one	one of the sticks
hook	one of the sticks	stick with a fork
forked stick	one of the sticks	one of the sticks
thin curved bamboo	piece of bamboo	curved bamboo
thin curved wood	one stick	one of the sticks
thin straight bamboo	one piece of bamboo	small bamboo
long fat bamboo	one of the bamboo	large bamboo
short thorny	one of the thorny	has a thorn
long thorny	one of the thorny sticks	has a thorn

[a]Note that actual order of presentation on Trial 2 was different from that of Trial 1.

It seems a fair description of our result to say that traditional rice farmers are poor communicators in a task where teacher and student (speaker and listener) do not share a common field of vision.

How are we to interpret this "fact"?

Interpreting Failures to Communicate

We can begin by noting that this communication-teaching situation is similar in many respects to experiments aimed at assessing the growth of cognitive development in children. The original motivation for this line of work came from studies by Piaget (1926) suggesting that young children have difficulty in understanding differences in points of view between themselves and people with whom they are talking (that is, they are egocentric).

In recent years, many investigators have extended Piaget's original observations to include procedures very similar to those we have just described. In one series of studies, Krauss and his associates found that as middle-class American children grow older, they produce shorter, more adequate descriptions of nonsense shapes. For example, a young child might say that a strangely shaped block "looks like my mother's hat," giving his listener no reliable clues to the identity of the object. Older children mention specific features of the object they are describing, which permit their listeners to make correct selections. (For a summary of this research see Glucksberg, Krauss, and Higgins, in press.)

This same technique has been used to explore population differences in the development of communicative skills. Krauss and Rotter (1968), Heider (1971), and several other investigators have rather consistently found performance differences among children from different socioeconomic and ethnic groups; children from lower socioeconomic groups perform more poorly than wealthier groups of children.

Although the exact theoretical terminology changes from one investigator to another, virtually everyone working in this field conceptualizes the source of the communicator's inadequacies as the result of a *failure to take into consideration the information the listener needs in order to understand the message.* This egocentrism of the child is most clearly seen, according to Piaget,

> when one child tries to explain something to another or in discussions among children. In both situations one sees the systematic difficulty children have in taking the point of view of the other, in making him grasp the desired information. . . . It is only after long training that the child reaches the point . . . where he speaks no longer for himself, but from the point of view of the other (Piaget and Inhelder, 1969, p. 122).

In terms of Piaget's theory, group differences in communicative performance reflect differences in the level of cognitive development achieved by the children in those groups. Piaget was, of course, speaking of groups defined by the children's age, but those who have studied ethnic and socioeconomic group differences have applied the same line of inference. In the early work of Bernstein (1970) and Krauss and Rotter (1968) it is hypothesized that lower-class children experience difficulties in such communication tasks (respond egocentrically) because of minimal interaction between child and adult and because lower-class speech patterns fail to make meanings explicit.

Summarizing this interpretative approach, we might want to conclude that for some reason (the nature of their language? the lack of formal schooling?) Kpelle adults are "egocentric"—that is, they have failed to develop the capacity to take a listener's point of view. Such an interpretation would represent an application of the experiment-as-thermometer point of view: the study measures egocentrism and Kpelle adults "have it."

Although this interpretation may seem plausible when applied to children 4, 5, or even 7 years old, is it reasonable to claim that the average Kpelle adult is no more developed cognitively than a Genevan first-grader, or that Kpelle speech patterns are inadequate for purposes of communication?

Our doubts about the reasonableness of this interpretation are quickly reinforced as soon as we step outside of the experimental situation—at just about the time our two subjects have talked us into buying them a bottle of beer! Our own, real-life, non-laboratory observations and the more controlled observations of many authropologists attest to the fact that there are no *generalized* problems of communication among traditional people.

Evans-Pritchard (1963), for example, describes the way in which the Zande people exploit the potential for ambiguity in speech in order to protect themselves against their supposedly hostile tribesmen. Here is a striking example of this form of indirect speech, called *sanza*:

> A man says in the presence of his wife to his friend, "friend, those swallows, how they flit about there." He is speaking about the flightiness of his wife and in case she should understand the allusion, he covers himself by looking up at the swallows as he makes his seemingly innocent remark. His friend understands what he means and replies, "yes, sir, do not talk to me about those swallows, how they come here, sir!" (What you say is only too true.) His wife also understands what he means and says tartly, "yes, sir, you leave that she (wife) to take a good she (wife), sir, since you married a swallow, sir!" (Marry someone else if that is the way you feel about it.) The husband looks surprised and pained that his wife would take umbrage at a harmless remark about swallows. He says to her, "does one get touchy about what is above (swallows), madam?" She replies, "Ai, sir. Deceiving me is not agreeable to me. You speak about me. You will fall from my tree." The sense of this reply is, "you are a fool to try and deceive me in my presence. It is me you speak about and you are always going at me. I will run away and something will happen to you when you try and follow me" (p. 211).

Evans-Pritchard's formulation for a successful *sanza* is as follows: "The great thing is to keep under cover and to keep open a line of retreat should the sufferer from your malice take offense and try to make trouble."

In order to be successful at this practice, the speaker must be very finely tuned in to the meaning ascribed to his remarks by the person he is addressing. If he cannot accurately assess the listener's point of view, he will be unable to carry the *sanza* through to its desired outcome.

Moreover, the speaker must take into consideration, not only the point of view of the listener, but also the point of view of others who may (intentionally) overhear part of the conversation. He must also consider various avenues of response open to the target of his malice and the culturally accepted rules that will protect him from such retaliation. In spite of these complex and difficult features of *sanza*, Evans-Pritchard find its use so effective and so ubiquitous in everyday Zande speech that our renowned Oxonian colleague is led to lament at the end of his article:

> It [sanza] adds greatly to the difficulties of anthropological inquiry. Eventually the anthropologist's sense of security is also undermined, his confidence shaken. He learns the language, can say what he wants to say in it, and can understand what he hears; but then he begins to wonder whether he has really understood . . . he cannot be sure, and even they [the Zande] cannot be sure, whether the words do have a nuance or someone imagines that they do.

He closes by quoting the Zande proverb, "Can one look into a person as one looks into an open-wove basket?" (P. 228.)

It is important to mention that while the particular form of ambiguous speech that Evans-Pritchard describes may have special features among the Zande, the use of rhetorical skills as a vehicle for controlling one's social environment is a very general feature of both nonliterate and literate societies (Albert, 1964; Labov, 1970).

Assuming the existence of such skills among the Kpelle—and there is good evidence for this assumption (Bellman, 1968)—the anthropological data on language usage seriously call into question the egocentrism interpretation of our Kpelle rice farmer's communication difficulties.

This interpretation is also challenged by observations of other cultural phenomena. Here a broader look at the developmental hypothesis first suggested by Piaget is useful; egocentric communication was not seen as an isolated phenomenon by Piaget, but as one manifestation of the intellectual organization of the young child.

In a recent summary, Piaget and Inhelder (1969) tell us that children who manifest egocentrism in their communication behavior also manifest it in the way they play games. When adults play games,

> there is common observance of the rules, which are known to the players; mutual surveillance to make sure the rules are observed; and above all, a collective spirit of honest competition, so that some win and others lose according to accepted rules (p. 119).

Young children play games quite differently:

> Everyone plays the game as he understands it, without much concern for or checking up on what the others are doing. . . . [M]ost significant, nobody loses and everybody wins at the same time, for the purpose is to have fun by playing for oneself while being stimulated by the group. . . . There is, then, a total lack of differentiation between social behavior and concentration on individual action (p. 119).

If Kpelle game-playing is supposed to reflect the same level of cognitive organization as their communication performance, we should look for childlike patterns of game play. Quite the opposite conclusions are suggested by the ethnographic literature on the Kpelle. As part of general descriptions of Kpelle life, several authors have presented evidence that the Kpelle play a variety of rule-governed games, adhering to modes of behavior that fit Piaget and Inhelder's characterization of *adult* gaming. Kulah (1973) describes a verbal game played according to strict rules, even by 6- to 7-year-old children. Cole and his associates (1971) went so far as to hold a tournament to determine the best adult players of a traditional Kpelle board game with complex rules. Some of the successful competitors were among the men who manifested inadequate responses in the communication task. Piaget and Inhelder also link communicative egocentrism to "children's initial difficulty in finding (even in seeking) modes of collaboration, as if collaboration did not constitute a specific end that must be pursued for its own sake" (p. 120).

Do the Kpelle generally experience difficulties in finding modes of cooperation? All the evidence we have (e.g., Gibbs, 1965) tells us just the opposite. Kpelle society has evolved a variety of institutions for ensuring cooperation among its members, for minimizing conflicts, and for maximizing the corporate good. Just one example of cooperative effort occurs in farming and housebuilding. For these enterprises, which require a lot of time and effort, people organize themselves into cooperative work groups, called *kuus*. As described by Bellman (1968), the operation of the *kuu* somewhat resembles a nineteenth-century barn raising. The common labor is accompanied by shared palm wine and shared music to make the work less oppressive. There may be competition involved (for example, to see who can cut the low bush most rapidly), but it is competition in the service of the corporate good.

In this, as in many other aspects of their lives, Kpelle adults seem to represent the antithesis of a Piagetian child.

From Negative to Positive: A Program of Research

Let us recapitulate what we have learned thus far.

1. Starting from anthropological observations that traditional, non-literate peoples do most of their learning and teaching in the context of the objects being discussed, we hypothesized that such people would experience problems if they had to communicate about objects not viewed in common.

2. We arranged a study that embodied our assumptions and found that difficulties in communication did in fact occur. Specifically, speakers did not tell listeners enough to permit unambiguous choices among objects.

3. We noted that when similar behavior is observed in young European and American children, it is attributed to their egocentrism—their inability to take another's point of view.

4. We pointed out that in other areas of cross-cultural research, psychological interpretations developed in Western cultures to explain experimental findings have often been uncritically accepted as explanations of similar findings in other cultures. In this vein, we asked whether the egocentricism interpretation of poor performance in the communication experiment could help us understand the outcome of the Kpelle study.

5. Turning to anthropological accounts of verbal behavior among the Kpelle and another tribal African group, we found these traditional people behaving in ways that we can interpret only by assuming that they do consider their listener's knowledge, and in very subtle ways. In behavior domains where the Piagetian theory tells us to expect further evidence of egocentrism, quite the opposite situation prevails.

It seems, in summary, as if our initial guess about communication difficulties was correct, but we are not much closer to specifying the mechanisms at work. Although we may agree that the research described thus far has been inadequate, the question remains: *Are* there any research strategies that will serve the purpose of helping us identify the process underlying poor (or competent) cognitive performance?

In order to increase our understanding of cultural influences on communication, three complementary courses of action suggest themselves.

First, we can systematically inquire into the task-specific sources of difficulty that the Kpelle speakers experience in the formal *experimental situation.* This calls for a research program in which we manipulate various features of the experiment so as to uncover the component processes involved in poor communication and to determine what particular conditions regulate which specific processes.

Second, we can follow up anthropological accounts with systematic investigation of the *situations in everyday life* in which the Kpelle show themselves to be good communicators. What distinguishes these situations from our laboratory (experimental) situation?

Third, we can return to the experiment to test specific hypotheses of what makes for good performance in naturally occuring situations. Through this back-and-forth process—from observation in natural settings to experiment in artificial or laboratory settings—we may be able to make progress in understanding the complex relations among cultural factors and communication.

In short, we are proposing that we tackle our problem through the twin methods of *experiment* (the psychologist's stock-in-trade) and *observation* (the anthropologist's specialty). We believe, and we hope to show, that these two methods, frequently considered unrelated if not actually antagonistic modes of inquiry, are instead complementary and mutually enriching research approaches. Let us consider each aspect of this visionary research program in turn.

Analyzing the Experiment

Some of the difficulties that may confront the Kpelle speaker in the communication experiment seem self-evident. For example, it is obvious that he must perceive the differences between the objects he is asked to describe and other similar objects in the array before him. If a speaker does not *see* or does not *notice* the differences among, say, the three bamboo sticks, he is not going to encode these differences for himself, let alone communicate them accurately.

A closely related hypothesis is that the necessary distinctions may be difficult to describe in the Kpelle language. Some basis for such speculation is provided by Gay and Cole (1967), who report the paucity of measurement terms that can be applied to materials like those used here.

Both these hypotheses are susceptible to experimental test, and indeed we have evidence concerning them. The possibility of linguistic deficiencies was ruled out in the 10-stick study just described, from which the example in Table 8–1 was drawn (Cole et al., 1969). This was accomplished by including a condition in which a college-educated Kpelle experimenter acted as the speaker. When this speaker described the sticks, his listeners made few errors in picking the correct alternative. Each of the necessary modifiers exists in Kpelle (long, short, thorny, and so forth) and when properly applied, they produced effective messages. This result also tells us that the Kpelle rice farmers *can* make the necessary perceptual distinctions among the sticks.

However, we still need to consider the possibility that our speakers, although capable of making the necessary perceptual discriminations, failed to do so because they did not *notice* the differences.

Several techniques suggest themselves as means of clarifying this issue. For example, we might begin the study by a preparatory session with the speaker in which we present him with pairs of sticks (thin curved bamboo and thin straight bamboo) and require him to tell us the difference between the two. In this way, we could assess each speaker's attention to, and encoding of, the discriminating attributes of the sticks.

We might get at the same set of issues by speculating along the following lines: Although Kpelle farmers are familiar with the sticks they are describing, their use of them rarely requires the kinds of discriminations required in this task. If we picked objects of equal complexity, but ones that embody culturally meaningful attributes, the speakers would spontaneously note them. For example, similar objects differing in their *functional* attributes might be more easily communicated (a hunting knife and a small knife for cutting vegetables). Perhaps objects with similar functions but of different manufacture would be more readily coded (a country-smelted cutlass and a store-bought, steel cutlass). A great many possibilities of this kind exist, all of which pursue the influence exerted on communication by the nature of the objects being communicated about.

This section would not be complete if we did not discuss the problems surrounding instructions to the subjects. This is a tricky issue because there are two interpretations of the claim that "the subjects did not know what to do": (1) The subjects were unclear about the goals and procedures of the experiment (what we ordinarily mean by instructions). And (2) they were not told what to do in order to accomplish the goal (which is usually the object of the study and not usually part of the instructions).

In the present communication study, a good deal of care was taken to make the instructions (the goals and procedures) clear. Preliminary instructions were tested with college-educated assistants, who prepared translations. The procedures were pilot-tested with Kpelle speakers who had not encountered the situation previously, and everyone *seemed* to understand what to do.

But the matter cannot be settled by any one "correct" set of instructions; the possibility of misunderstanding still exists. The only reasonable course is to conduct a study that incorporates instructional variations that eliminate specific sources of misunderstanding.

For example, in the 10-sticks experiment, instead of laying the sticks in two piles and simply telling the subjects that pairs of sticks are supposed to be matched, the experimenter might lay out the sticks as they should appear when matched, so that subjects could see the desired outcome.

A second instructional approach is to give the subjects repeated practice with one or more sets of materials. In the study we have been discussing, subjects were shown the outcome of their choices after the first trial, and the speaker did improve his messages, as Table 8–1 indicates. From our point of view, the repeated trials constitute practice, but the nature of this practice is instructional in that it has the effect of making clear to the speaker just what is required of him.

This practice, or training, approach is also directly relevant to evaluating alternative hypotheses about the source of a speaker's inadequacies. According to the egocentrism hypothesis (even if it is applicable only in this limited context), the speaker *cannot* take the point of view of his listener. Therefore, if practice in the task leads to improvement, the egocentrism hypothesis has to be weakened, at least to the extent of claiming that the speaker *can* take into account the listener's point of view, even though he does not.

Studies in the United States (summarized in Glucksberg et al., in press) do *not* find practice effects in children younger than 8 years, but they have found practice effects in children over 8, thus supporting the notion that the younger children are *unable* to handle the task. In Table 8–1 we see clear improvement in the performance of the speaker (although it is by no means perfect). This finding supports the idea that more precise instructions (here embodied in the correction procedure) will reveal communicative competence where we had thought it absent.

Investigating Naturally Occurring Situations

A series of studies modeled along the lines described in the previous section would certainly increase our understanding of the conditions under which traditional Kpelle rice farmers will or will not produce adequate messages for unseen listeners in a particular species of experimental situation. But to restrict our inquiry in this way is to lose sight of our original research goal, which is to specify the relation between culturally determined experiences and communicative (teaching and learning) behavior.

A necessary complementary approach is suggested by the anthropological observations we have summarized above.

To begin with, can we pinpoint, in those communication situations where anthropological evidence suggests that speakers *do* seem to take into account their listener's point of view, any factor or factors that distinguish those situations from our experimental situation, where the speakers do not consider the listener's point of view?

The obvious first candidate is exactly the variable we picked as the focus of our interest—whether or not the speaker and listener can make face-to-face contact with each other.

Starting again from this point, we might be tempted to choose a commonly occurring face-to-face communication situation, just to make sure that "anthropological wisdom" about the nonverbal nature of the teaching in such societies is correct. Among the Kpelle, for instance, we might ask a skilled basket maker to teach a novice how to weave a basket and simply record the proceedings. John Gay reports, in a personal communication, that he has made such observations in an informal way, and he confirms that the teacher relies heavily on demonstration ("you do it like this"). Moreover, the few teachers sampled seemed to have difficulty in describing the total process when explicitly asked to do so.

We might now be led to wonder what would happen if someone were asked to teach about an object for which no long-standing teaching techniques had been established.

For example, many people in Kpelle-land now carry flashlights, yet few know how to take a flashlight apart, and put it back together. What would happen if we selected a group of Kpelle adults and gave them an elementary knowledge of flashlights— the names of their components, how they are put together, and how to determine the source of malfunctions? Then, in individual sessions, each teacher could be asked to teach another adult what he had learned. Motivation for good performance could be insured by rewarding successful teachers and students with flashlights. The question then becomes: Will teachers apply a traditional demonstration teaching technique, or will they provide verbal descriptions and elaborations of the sort they themselves received?

Extensions of this line of inquiry would lead us to ask people to instruct friends or strangers about the directions to a distant town, in order to see whether the speakers modified their instructions to suit the knowledge of the listener. We might ask people to describe themselves so that someone from another village could pick them out from a group of their friends, to see whether they would pick adequate descriptions. In general, we could devise a variety of naturalistic and quasi-experimental observations that would tell us a good deal more about habitual teaching techniques as well as about the conditions under which people seem to take a listener's point of view into account.

Integrating Experiment and Observation

Based on what we learn, we could try to test specific hypotheses about conditions for effective communication in the formalized setting of the experiment. We might begin by devising a situation like the communication experiment, with a speaker who describes to a listener each of a set of objects, like sticks. We would, however, preserve the natural feature of social communication by allowing the two participants to be in face-to-face contact.

Although this is a simple enough proposal, there are many practical hurdles to overcome, especially in primitive field situations.

Consider what would happen if we simply removed the barrier between the two men. When the experimenter selected a stick from the pile and laid it down, the speaker would not have to say a word; the listener could simply look over his pile of sticks and pick the matching one.

A slightly more plausible idea might be to conduct the study as follows: The speaker and listener sit across a table from each other, but only the *listener* has a pile of sticks in front of him. The matching 10 sticks are held by the experimenter, who is seated behind the listener, where the speaker can see him but the listener cannot. The experimenter holds up one stick at a time, and the speaker must verbally instruct the listener so that he will pick out the corresponding stick.

This procedure could produce a variety of outcomes, depending on whether the listener is allowed to ask questions, on whether the speaker is permitted to modify his directions if he sees the listener making an incorrect choice, and also on the kinds of verbal instructions that are allowable. Even posing the problem in this manner suggests some of the factors operating in real-life communication which we did not permit in our original experiment. Suppose that a speaker says, "the bamboo one," and the listener dutifully picks one of the three bamboo sticks but not the correct one. If allowed to respond in any way he deems appropriate, the speaker might point to the correct one, or say, "no, not that one, the other one over there." But supposing that we do not permit the speaker to point, a variety of nondescriptive responses could still be used to guide the listener.

Several versions of letting things run their natural course (perhaps even to the extent of allowing pointing) would be a reasonable first step, but would not capture the spirit of the experimental communication task. So we could add increasingly stringent restrictions, such as "you can't point," "you can only give one message for each stick," and so on. In this way we could determine exactly which components are crucial to adequate communication.

It would be possible to continue the list of relevant experiments on the problem of culture and communication, but it is not our intent to display the extent of our experimental imaginations or to try the reader's endurance. We have gone into some detail in the previous sections in order to suggest the kind of experimental program that is necessary if we are to provide a rich and convincing account of the relation between cultural variations and variations in communicative performance. Assuming that still other questions need to be asked if we are to reach something approaching real understanding, we want to return now to the principles underlying the approach to culture and cognition that this example illustrates.

Cognitive Differences

The example of a research program on communication skills and their cultural variations has pitted two points of view against each other—the more standard view that cultural differences in cognition are composed largely of differences in the existence or amount of some hypothetical psychological capacity (egocentrism, for example) and the view that such differences reside in the way particular processes are brought to bear on the problem at hand. At the beginning of this chapter, we used a theoretical argument to assert that it is not useful to conceive of cognition in terms of capacities or properties or characteristics. The communication experiment example demonstrates that, in *practice*, such a view leads to unresolvable ambiguities and paradoxes in the interpretation of experimental data and their integration with the research findings of anthropologists. We suggested that conceptualizing cognition in terms of *processes* or *operations* might help us develop research that would be more fruitful in locating the specific sources of observed differences in performance.

The communication experiment and our analysis of it suggest that a variety of related cognitive processes have to operate together in the experimental situation for effective communication to occur. Successful formulation of a message was seen to require the speaker to *perceive* differences among the sticks, to *attend* to distinctive, distinguishing features of the stimuli, to *assign* appropriate descriptive terms from his vocabulary, to *remember* descriptions already used, and to *understand* the task at hand. Virtually every area of cognition described in this book plays some part in successful communication performance. And we have not yet listed the ability to take the point of view of the listener!

It seems clear to us that a failure in any one of these processes, either because the person "does not have it" or because he fails to apply it, can yield poor performance.

This is not a new point of view in psychology, although it is one that has not received much attention in Western European and American writing. However, in the early 1920s a very similar position was advanced by L. S. Vygotsky. Speaking in the context of the cortical representation of complex cognitive processes, A. R. Luria, Vygotsky's student, has repeatedly asserted that "higher mental functions are complex, organized *functional systems*," the components of which are represented in different areas of the brain and combined in different constellations depending on the task at hand (see Luria, 1966, pp. 23ff). Furthermore, Luria emphasizes that neither the components nor the functional relations into which they enter are already formed at birth. Rather, they are formed in the course of each individual's development and depend very closely on the social experiences of the child.

As an illustration of a functional system, we can consider the set of experiments on free recall discussed in Chapter 6. In those studies, it was consistently found that educated and noneducated subjects performed differently. In tracing the source of the differences, we saw that under some circumstances, both groups showed efficient, organized recall. However, under standard experimental situations, the groups without schooling did not recall well, did not improve much with repeated practice, and did not organize their recall categorially. Yet, as the work of Scribner (unpublished) demonstrates, taxonomic categorization entered into the performance of both educated and noneducated subjects. It did not, however, play the same role in the recall of the two groups. For the noneducated groups it was present (as seen in the way items were grouped prior to recall) but did not play a controlling role in the recall process itself. For the educated groups, taxonomic categorization was both the dominant mode of sorting the stimuli and the control mechanism in recall. In the language of functional systems, we would say that the same component has entered into two different functional systems (those characteristic of the educated and noneducated groups for this task) and it is the *functional systems* that differ.

Another way to look at this is to say that the same component process may play different roles, depending on the organized functional system of which it is a part. In the case of the educated subjects, their categorization of the material *led* their recall, while with the villagers it played an *auxiliary* role (which we are not yet in a position to characterize more precisely). For certain tasks, one functional system may be more effective—that is, may produce better performance—than another. In some situations, however, equal levels of performance might be achieved by different functional systems. The recall of a set of objects that has been sorted into groups might be mediated by visual representation of the objects, by the names of individual items or names of the groups into which they have been sorted ("things we hunt with"), or by different combinations of these representational processes— all of which might produce the same outcome. *Whether or not the outcome is the same,* the important research problem for the psychologist is to identify the processes actually employed by different subjects and to determine how these processes were coordinated to handle the task at hand. We are conceiving of functional systems, then, as flexible and variable organizations of cognitive processes directed toward some fixed end.

A major implication of this view for cross-cultural work is that *we are unlikely to find cultural differences in basic component cognitive processes.* While we cannot completely rule out this possibility, there is no evidence, in any line of investigation that we have reviewed, that any cultural group wholly lacks a basic process such as abstraction, or inferential reasoning, or categorization. Rather, the data have left us to wrestle with the problem of why it is that some procedures suggest that a given process is involved in the performance and some suggest it is not. The concept of functional system is helpful here. We might start with the hypothesis that sociocultural factors play an important role in influencing which of possible alternative processes (visual or verbal representation, for example) are evoked in a given situation and what role they play in the total performance (is verbal encoding used in the active process of rehearsal in a memory task or not?). To illustrate again with our communication example: it may be that Kpelle adults in the domain of social intercourse adopt the orientation of the other person but that this orientation is not activated when the task at hand is transmitting information about impersonal, technical matters such as, in the experimental case, object properties. If cultural differences are assumed to be reflected in the way functional systems are organized for various purposes, then a double line of research becomes important: the first is to uncover the culturally determined experiential factors that give rise to different dominant functional systems (is formal schooling the critical experience for the development of techniques of categorized recall in the free-recall experiment?); the second is to determine which situational features—content domain, task requirements—call out which functional organizations.

Nothing we have said so far can be considered a theory of culture and cognition—not even a primitive one! But we think the concept of *functional cognitive systems*, which may vary with cultural variations, may be a most useful approach to guide future research and may at some point offer the possibility of an eventual integration of theory and fact in this field.

From a research point of view, this approach highlights several needs. Greater attention needs to be paid to the possible range of cultural features that may be implicated in the development of certain modal functional systems (we will return to this point later). We also need to isolate general dimensions of task situations that are related to differences in behavior. Demonstrating that there are variations in the situations within which people manifest a particular cognitive process may be a good beginning, but it is not psychologically meaningful unless we can specify the rules underlying the patterns of behavior that we see in different situations. Clearly a part of any situation-dependent theory is going to have to include a theory of situations. No such theory exists, and none is likely to be developed without the close participation of cultural anthropologists.

From the functional systems point of view, which we have been espousing, it readily follows that our insistence on a variety of approaches to studying a particular kind of cognitive performance is neither a caprice nor an effort to garner a large number of publications. It is an absolute requirement, dictated by our conception of the origin and organization of cognitive processes.

This idea, that single experiments are inadequate for the evaluation of culture–cognition hypotheses, is widely recognized even by those who tend to theorize in very different terms. Many authors have written on this subject, but the classic statement was made by Donald Campbell (1961):

> We who are interested in using such [cross-cultural] data for delineating process rather than exhaustively describing single instances must accept this rule: *No comparison of a single pair of natural objects is interpretable* . . . (p. 344).
>
> However, if there are multiple indicators which vary in their irrelevant attributes, and if these all agree as to the direction of the difference on the theoretically intended aspects, then the number of rival explanations becomes greatly reduced and the confirmation of theory more nearly certain (p. 345).

Looking back at the research programs described in previous chapters, we can see that the most compelling lines of research followed Campbell's prescription, at least in part. For example, the extensive series of studies by Dawson and Berry on cultural variations in field-dependence would have little plausibility if they had been restricted to two cultural groups and a single experimental task (say, Temme versus Scots on the embedded figures test). The hypothesis that child-rearing and ecological factors combine to influence the degree of field-independence gained considerable plausibility from the fact that the pattern of relationships appeared over several different cultural groups and two or more seemingly unrelated tasks, such as the embedded figures test and Hudson's test of three-dimensional picture perception (as described in the work of Berry, 1971).

However, our requirements for a successful research program go beyond the recommendations of Campbell, and far beyond the practice of Berry and others, in the range and number of observations that we ordinarily think of as necessary in order to confirm a cross-cultural hypothesis. Although Campbell would almost certainly agree to the usefulness of the experimental program that we laid out in connection with our hypothesis about culture and communication, his remarks have almost always been applied within the context of rather narrowly defined experimental operations; nowhere are there suggestions for making observations akin to watching traditional teachers at work or analyzing the content of an exchange of verbal insults. Where anthropological variables do enter into the experimental programs we have been

reviewing, they have most often occurred in the search for interesting populations among whom a test or experiment should be
tried. This is the strategy used in the Berry research just mentioned.

We have seen, however, that it is enormously difficult to interpret any set of experimental data, no matter how well conceived
and elaborated the experimental program, without taking into
account knowledge about the culture and the behavior of the
people gained from the work of anthropologists, linguists, and
other social scientists. While it is important to integrate general
knowledge from the various intellectual disciplines, we would go
further in suggesting that the *methods* of these relevant fields of
endeavor need to be integrated for the purpose of generating information on particular hypotheses. Field and laboratory, anthropological observation and psychological experimentation, can
yield knowledge from different perspectives about the same function. In outlining our model research program on communication,
for example, we showed that naturalistic observations of traditional teaching methods could be important in generating specific
hypotheses about communication behavior and in helping us pinpoint what there is about the experimental situation that dis-
rupts effective communication patterns. The idea that different
disciplines should cooperate in an integrated research program is
certainly not new. A number of cooperative endeavors have been
carried out in studies of culture and personality and of cultural
variations in socialization practices. But, as we have seen, such
examples are unhappily still rare in cross-cultural investigations
of cognition.

Another research implication of the functional-systems view
is that wherever possible in the design of cross-cultural experiments (as opposed to other types of observation) all kinds of
performance ought to be readily interpretable in terms of what
the person *is* doing. This point follows directly from our criticisms
of the way that psychologists interpret lack of performance, but
it is by no means easy to implement. Still it is worth mentioning
because cleverly designed experiments can shorten the string of
observations necessary to make decisions about a hypothesis.

As a positive example of what we mean, we can mention the
experiment by Deregowski (see Chapter 4) in which he was
evaluating the role of the perspective of the viewer and the per-

spective of the photographer in situations where the two did not coincide. This was not, strictly speaking, a cross-cultural experiment, since Deregowski was trying to track down the source of errors in the perceptual performance of a particular African nonliterate group. But the example is useful because he did not pose his hypothesis in terms of success or failure, but in terms of subjects' adherence to one of two viewing perspectives. It could have turned out, of course, that his subjects adopted neither perspective and the pattern of results could not have been directly interpretable, but the chance of such an outcome was minimized by the nature of his experimental design. Since he was able to interpret performance in terms of what subjects *did*, he could then follow up with a meaningful question about cultural influences by asking, "And how does Group X respond to this task?" In a more limited way the studies of free recall have proved useful because hypotheses about different memory strategies (rote recapitulation versus meaningful reorganization) could be tested directly from the data. Unhappily, that series of experiments is notable for the fact that subjects failed to respond consistently with either hypothesis, necessitating the long and still-incomplete series of experiments that followed.

Cultural Differences

At numerous points in this volume we have commented on the fact that the overwhelming majority of cross-cultural psychological experiments consist essentially of finding two populations that contrast in some theoretically interesting way, and then running a standardized test on the two groups to see whether there is a difference in performance.

Yet it may be noticed that in our extended discussion of hypotheses about communication among the Kpelle, no mention was made of studies contrasting children of different ages, schoolchildren and nonliterate children, adults involved in special activities, or any of a number of seemingly interesting contrasts of this general type.

Of course, we did have, in the back of our minds, a general contrast between traditional Kpelle farmers and *someone* (what else could cross-cultural mean?), and we did mention the fact that American third-graders did not experience difficulties with the experimental task we presented the farmers. But the key point is that an entire experimental program was generated without intergroup comparisons at its center.

How could this be?

We think it arises from two characteristics of our view toward psychological research on cognition.

Partly as a result of believing in our own criticism of the research we have been reviewing, and partly as a result of adopting a functional-systems approach to the study of culture and cognition, we have come to a new view of the role of intergroup comparisons: Instead of a useful way to *test* cross-cultural hypotheses, we find that intergroup comparisons of the sort typically encountered (educated and noneducated, middle class and lower class, hunters and farmers, indulgent upbringers and disciplinarians) seem to function more as *hypothesis generators*. In every chapter of this book, a study that was intended to test a hypothesis about culture and cognition gave rise to much deeper speculations about the actual mechanisms involved in the particular performance *in any culture*. We were led to speculate about the many things a person needs to learn in order to interpret or copy a picture, the many stages between presentation and recall of a list of unconnected words, the factors that control whether someone puts two and two together to make an apparently simple inference, and so on. In each of these cases, the fact that one group performs well while another group seems to experience severe difficulties becomes a stimulus to the investigator to re-examine his ideas of what good performance entails—so long as he does not conclude that poor performance implies a corresponding lack of process. In a very real sense, cross-cultural experimentation conducted in this spirit can add as much to our knowledge of ourselves as it adds to our knowledge of "them."

Intergroup comparisons, however, can and should be made to help illuminate the factors that lead to the *development* of different organizations of cognitive functions. The kind of intergroup comparisons that are likely to be most helpful are comparisons of groups *within the same culture*. As we have become familiar with the details of research programs, we cannot fail to have been impressed by the fact that the old simplistic notion of some generic entity called "primitive culture" has given way to an appreciation of the diversity of traditional *cultures*. Beyond this, we have seen that the population within a *single* traditional culture—even one with a low technological level and little differentiation of labor—does not constitute a homogenous mass such that one can talk about *the* Temne or *the* Kpelle for all purposes without taking into consideration the fact that some Temne are hunters, some not; that some Kpelle are farmers, others are blacksmiths, and in greatly expanding numbers some today are factory workers. Populations within cultures may be differentiated by all the characteristics popularly used in psychological research in the United States: age, sex, and the like. New and exciting research opportunities present themselves in third-world countries, however; many of the societies are undergoing rapid change, and these changing circumstances are affecting different segments of the population. Thus it becomes possible to investigate the effects of schooling on apparently comparable groups of children from the same village (as Greenfield did), or the effects of modernization of village life on adults still involved in traditional occupations (as Scribner did).

Traditional cultures in transition would thus seem to offer an important natural laboratory in which to explore the historical factors (from a societal point of view) and the developmental factors (from an individual point of view) which contribute to specific cognitive organizations. To pursue such questions would call upon still another research strategy—one rarely made use of in cross-cultural research. That is the longitudinal research design, which follows one group of people through time to see what changes in life experiences may lead to changes in cognitive skills. Same-group comparisons at two points of time within a culture might usefully complement intergroup comparisons at one point of time. Neither inter-group, nor same-group, nor two-or-more-culture comparisons have special powers, however; each is but one tool in the psychologist's kit, a tool that is not useful taken by itself, but only when used in conjunction with others.

By now it must be evident that our aim in this book is not to mark out a new *field* of psychology. Rather, we want to encourage a new *approach* to the study of the role of culture in psychological development. We have touched briefly on the main features of this approach in the present chapter and they have been evident in the questions we raised and conclusions we drew from the research reviewed throughout the book. At the heart of this approach is a commitment to pursue a program of research that attempts to integrate in theory and in practice the knowledge and methods of *both* anthropology and psychology. It implies that the truly challenging questions about human thought and its development will only yield to inquiry when investigators bring to bear on them all the tools that the separate sciences have developed for studying man-in-his-culture.

A Final Word: Experimenters and Their Points of View

Discussions of scientific method in psychology emphasize the need to put psychological theory and experimentation on a rigorous, scientific plane. A good deal of attention is devoted to *method*—the rules by which experiments are designed, subjects are selected, stimuli are equated, and data are analyzed. This book has contributed its fair share to such a discussion.

Nonetheless, we hope it does not escape the reader's attention that in this last chapter, extraordinary weight has been placed on the role of the experimenter's point of view in insuring the success of the scientific enterprise. The really influential psychological theories dominating cognitive psychology today (Piaget's theory is a good example) have not gained their influence through the prediction of one or two unusual phenomena, or the specification of a single, unanticipated relationship. Rather, they have convinced us by repeated successes in a wide variety of situations within our own culture. But carrying such theories overseas without some awareness of their cultural roots and their very real limitations, even in the cultures in which they arose, carries with it the risk of experimental egocentrism—mistaking as universals the particular organizations of cognitive skills that have arisen in the historical circumstances of our own society, and interpreting their absence in other cultures as "deficiency." Perhaps this risk may never be entirely overcome until psychological science in non-Western countries becomes further advanced and generates its own theories and research methods—which can be tested on us!

It is well to remember that all of the processes and problems that we encounter in the people we study apply to us as experimenters. The future of the study of culture and cognition will depend upon our abilities to organize our own functional systems to give a comprehensive and coherent account of the intellectual behaviors of those whom we so provincially refer to as "our subjects."

I know how to begin the old mat pattern but I do not know how to begin the new.

An old Kpelle proverb

References

Albert, E. M. "Rhetoric," "logic," and "poetics" in Burundi: culture patterning of speech behavior. *American Anthropologist*, 1964, *66*, 35–54.

Allport, G. W., & Pettigrew, T. F. Cultural influences on the perception of movement: the trapezoidal illusion among Zulus. *Journal of Abnormal and Social Psychology*, 1957, *55*, 104–113.

Ames, A., Jr. Visual perception and the rotating trapezoidal window. *Psychological Monographs*, 1951, *65*, Whole No. 324.

Asch, S. E. The metaphor: a psychological inquiry. In M. Henle, *Documents of Gestalt psychology*. Berkeley: University of California Press, 1961, 324–333.

Baihdurashvili, A. G. Summarized in report of the Fourth Congress of the Psychological Society of the USSR. *Soviet Psychology*, 1972, *X*, 359–423.

Bartlett, F. C. *Psychology and primitive culture*. Cambridge University Press, 1923. Reprint. Westport, Conn.: Greenwood Press, 1970.

Bartlett, F. C. *Remembering*. London: Cambridge University Press, 1932.

Bartlett, F. C. *Thinking*. New York: Basic Books, 1958.

Bellman, B. L. Field notes. January 10, 1968.

Bentley, W. H. Pioneering on the Congo. Quoted in R. Allier, *The mind of the savage*. New York: Harcourt Brace, 1929.

Berlin, B., & Kay, P. *Basic color terms*. Berkeley: University of California Press, 1969.

Bernstein, B. A sociolinguistic approach to socialization: with some reference to educability. In F. Williams, *Language and poverty*. Chicago: Markham Publishing Co., 1970.

Bernstein, B. Social class, language, and socialization. In S. Moscovici (Ed.), *The psychosociology of language*. Chicago: Markham Publishing Co., 1972, 222–242.

Berry, J. W. Temme and Eskimo perceptual skills. *International Journal of Psychology*, 1966, *1* (3), 207–229.

Berry, J. W. Ecology and socialization as factors in figural assimilation and the resolution of binocular rivalry. *International Journal of Psychology*, 1969, *4*, 271–280.

Berry, J. W. Müller-Lyer susceptibility. Culture, ecology or race? *International Journal of Psychology*, 1971, *6*, 193–197 (a).

Berry, J. W. Ecological and cultural factors in spatial perceptual development. *Canadian Journal of Behavioral Science*, 1971, *3*, (4), 324–336 (b).

Boas, F. *The mind of primitive man.* 1911. Reprint. New York: The Free Press, 1965.

Boring, E. G. *A history of experimental psychology.* Second edition. New York: Appleton-Century-Crofts, 1950.

Bornstein, M. H. The psychophysiological component of cultural difference in color naming and illusion susceptibility. *Behavor Science Notes*, 1973, *8*, 41–101.

Bousfield, W. A. The occurrence of clustering in the free recall of randomly arranged associates. *Journal of General Psychology*, 1953, *49*, 229–240.

Bowen, E. *Return to laughter.* New York: Doubleday, 1954.

Brimble, A. R. The construction of a nonverbal intelligence test in northern Rhodesia. *Journal of the Rhodes-Livingstone Institute*, Dec. 1963, *34*, 23–35.

Brown, R. *Words and things.* New York: The Free Press, 1958.

Brown, R., Black, A. H., & Horowits, A. E. Phonetic symbolism in natural language. *Journal of Abnormal and Social Psychology*, 1955, *50*, 388–393.

Brown, R., & Lenneberg, E. H. A study of language and cognition. *Journal of Abnormal and Social Psychology*, 1954, *49*, 454–462.

Bruner, J. S., Olver, R., & Greenfield, P. *Studies in cognitive growth.* New York: Wiley, 1966.

Bunzel, R. L. Introduction. In L. Levy-Bruhl, *How natives think.* New York: Washington Square Press, 1966.

Burnham, R. W., & Clark, J. R. A test of hue memory. *Journal of Applied Psychology*, 1955, *39*, 164–172.

Campbell, D. T. The mutual methodological relevance of anthropology and psychology. In F. L. K. Hsu (Ed.), *Psychological anthropology.* Homewood, Ill.: Dorsey Press, 1961, 333–352.

Carroll, J. B., & Casagrande, J. B. The function of language classifications in behavior. In E. E. Macoby, T. M. Newcomb, & E. L. Hartley (Eds.), *Readings in social psychology.* New York: Holt, Rinehart and Winston, 1958.

Castaneda, C. *The teachings of Don Juan: a Yaqui way of knowledge.* New York: Ballantine Books, 1968.

Chamberlain, A. F. *The child: a study in the evolution of man.* London: Walter Scott, 1901.

Chomsky, N. *Language and mind.* New York: Harcourt, Brace & World, 1968.

Cofer, C. Does conceptual clustering influence the amount retained in immediate free recall? In B. Klienmuntz (Ed.), *Concepts and the structure of memory.* New York: Wiley, 1967.

Cole, M., Frankel, F., & Sharp, D. W. The development of free recall learning in children. *Developmental Psychology*, 1971, *4*, 109–123.

Cole, M., & Gay, J. Culture and memory. *American Anthropologist,* 1972, *74* (5), 1066–1084.

Cole, M., Gay, J., & Glick, J. Communication skills among the Kpelle of Liberia. Paper presented at the Society for Research in Child Development Meeting, Santa Monica, Calif., March 1969.

Cole, M., Gay, J., Glick, J., & Sharp, D. W. Linguistic structure and transposition. *Science,* 1969, *164,* 90–91.

Cole, M., Gay, J., Glick, J., & Sharp, D. W. *The cultural context of learning and thinking.* New York: Basic Books, 1971.

Dasen, P. R. Cross-cultural Piagetian research: a summary. *Journal of Cross-Cultural Psychology,* 1972, *3,* 23–39.

Dasen, P. R. The influence of ecology, culture and European contact on cognitive development in Australian Aborigines. In J. W. Berry & P. R. Dasen (Eds.), *Culture and cognition: readings in cross-cultural psychology.* London: Methuen, 1973.

Dawson, J. L. M. Cultural and physiological influences upon spatial-perceptual processes in West Africa, Part I. *International Journal of Psychology,* 1967, *2,* 115–128.

D'Azevedo, W. The uses of the past in Gola discourse. *Journal of African History,* 1962, *1,* 11–34.

deLacey, P. R. A cross-cultural study of classificatory ability in Australia. *Journal of Cross-Cultural Psychology,* 1970, *1,* 293–304.

de Lemos, M. M. The development of conservation in Aboriginal children. *International Journal of Psychology,* 1969, *4,* 255–269.

Deregowski, J. B. Pictorial recognition in subjects from a relatively pictureless environment. *African Social Research,* 1968, *5,* 356–364 (a).

Deregowski, J. B. Difficulties in pictorial depth perception in Africa. *British Journal of Psychology,* 1968, *59,* 195–204 (b).

Deregowski, J. B. On perception of depicted orientation. *International Journal of Psychology,* 1968, *3,* 149–156 (c).

Deregowski, J. B. Effect of cultural value of time upon recall. *British Journal of Social and Clinical Psychology,* 1970, *9,* 37–41.

Deregowski, J. B., & Serpell, R. Performance on a sorting task with various modes of representation: a cross-cultural experiment. Human Development Research Unit, University of Zambia, Report No. 18, 1971 (Mimeographed).

Duncker, K. On problem solving. *Psychological Monographs,* 1945, *58* (5). Whole No. 270.

Elkind, D. Conservation and concept formation. In D. Elkind & J. Flavell (Eds.), *Studies in cognitive developoment.* New York: Oxford University Press, 1969, 171–190.

Evans-Pritchard, E. E. *Essays in social anthropology.* New York: Free Press of Glencoe, 1963.

Evreux, Y. *Voyage dans le nord du Brēsil fait durant les annēes 1613 et 1614.* Paris and Leipzig: A Franck, 1864. (Human Relations Area Files: New Haven, Conn.)

Fishman, J. A systematization of the Whorfian hypothesis. *Behavioral Science,* 1960, *5,* 323–339.

Fortes, M. Education in Taleland. *Africa,* 1938, *XI* (Supplement), 4.

Gay, J. Kpelle uses of Kpelle logic. *Liberian Research Association Journal,* 1971, *4.*

Gay, J., & Cole, M. *The new mathematics and an old culture.* New York: Holt, Rinehart & Winston, 1967.

Gibbs, J. The Kpelle of Liberia. In J. Gibbs (Ed.), *Peoples of Africa.* New York: Holt, Rinehart and Winston, 1965.

Ginsburg, H., & Opper, S. *Piaget's theory of intellectual development: an introduction.* Englewood Cliffs, N.J.: Prentice-Hall, 1969.

Gladwin, T. *East is a big bird.* Cambridge, Mass.: Belknap Press, 1970.

Glucksberg, S., Krauss, R. M., & Higgins, E. T. The development of referential communication skills. In F. Horowitz & G. Siegal, *Review of child development,* 1973.

Goldstein, K., & Scheerer, M. Abstract and concrete behavior. *Psychological Monographs,* 1941, *53* (239).

Goodenough, F. L. The measurement of mental functions in primitive groups. *American Anthropologist,* 1936, *38,* 1–11.

Goodnow, J. J. Research on culture and thought. In D. Elkind & J. H. Flavell (Eds.), *Studies in cognitive development.* New York, London: Oxford University Press, 1969.

Goodnow, J., & Bethon, G. Piaget's tasks: the effects of schooling and intelligence. *Child Development,* 1966, *37,* 573–582.

Greenberg, J. Language universals. In T. A. Sebeok (Ed.), *Current trends in linguistics,* Vol. 3. The Hague: Mouton, 1966.

Greenfield, P. M., & Bruner, J. S. Culture and cognitive growth. In D. A. Goslin (Ed.), *Handbook of socialization theory and research.* New York: Rand McNally, 1969.

Hall, G. S. In C. Strickland & C. Burgess (Eds.), *Health, growth and heredity.* New York: Teachers College Press, 1965.

Harris, M. *The rise of anthropological theory.* New York: Crowell, 1968.

Havelock, E. A. *Preface to Plato.* Cambridge: Balknap Press, Harvard University Press, 1963.

Heider, E. R. Style and accuracy of verbal communications within and between social classes. *Journal of Personality and Social Psychology,* 1971, *18,* 33–47.

Heider, E. R. Universals in color naming and memory. *Journal of Experimental Psychology,* 1972, *93,* 10–20.

Heider, E. R., & Olivier, D. C. The structure of the color space in naming and memory for two languages. *Cognitive Psychology*, 1972, *3*, 337–355.

Henle, M. On the relation between logic and thinking. *Psychological Review*, 1962, *69*, 366–378.

Heron, A. Concrete operations, "g" and achievement in Zambian children. *Journal of Cross-Cultural Psychology*, 1971, *2*, 325–336.

Herskovits, M. Foreword. In F. Boas, *The mind of primitive man*. New York: The Free Press, 1965 (revised edition).

Hockett, C. Chinese versus English: an exploration of the Whorfian theses. In H. Hoijer (Ed.), *Language in culture*. Chicago: University of Chicago Press, 1954.

Hudson, W. Pictorial depth perception in sub-cultural groups in Africa. *Journal of Social Psychology*, 1960, *52*, 183–208.

Hudson, W. Cultural problems in pictorial perception. *South African Journal of Science*, 1962, *58* (7), 189–195 (a).

Hudson, W. Pictorial perception and educational adaptation in Africa. *Psychologica Africana*, 1962, *9*, 226–239 (b).

Hudson, W. The study of the problem of pictorial perception among un-acculturated groups. *International Journal of Psychology*, 1967, *2*, 89–107.

Irwin, M. H., & Mclaughlin, D. H. Ability and preference in category sorting by Mano schoolchildren and adults. *Journal of Social Psychology*, 1970, *82*, 15–24.

Jahoda, G. Geometric illusions and environment: a study in Ghana. *British Journal of Psychology*, 1966, *57*, 193–199.

Jahoda, G. Retinal pigmentation, illusion susceptibility and space perception. *International Journal of Psychology*, 1971, *6*, 99–208.

Kamin, L. J. Heredity, intelligence, politics and psychology. Presented at Eastern Psychological Association, Washington, D.C., May 1973.

Kendler, T. S., & Kendler, H. H. Experimental analysis of inferential behavior in children. In L. P. Lipsitt & C. C. Spiker (Eds.), *Advances in child development and behavior*, Vol. 3. New York: Academic Press, 1967.

Kendler, T. S., Kendler, H. H., & Carrick, M. The effect of verbal labels on inferential problem solution. *Child Development*, 1966, *37*, 749–763.

Klank, L. J. K., Huang, Y. H., & Johnson, R. C. Determinants of success in matching word pairs in tests of phonetic symbolism. *Journal of Verbal Learning and Verbal Behavior*, 1971, *10*, 140–148.

Köhler, W. The mentality of apes. New York: Harcourt Brace, 1925.

Köhler, W. Psychological remarks on some questions of anthropology. In M. Henle (Ed.), *Documents of Gestalt psychology*. Berkeley: University of California Press, 1961.

Krauss, R. M., & Rotter, G. S. Communication abilities of children as a function of status and age. *The Merrill-Palmer Quarterly*, April 1968, *14*, 161–173.

Kulah, A. The organization and learning of proverbs among the Kpelle of Liberia. Unpublished doctoral dissertation, University of California, Irvine, 1973.

Labov, W. The logic of nonstandard English. In F. Williams, *Language and poverty*. Chicago: Markham Publishing Co., 1970.

Lantz, D., & Stefflre, V. Language and cognition revisited. *Journal of Abnormal and Social Psychology*, 1964, *69*, 472–481.

Lee, D. Conceptual implications of an Indian language. *Philosophy of Science*, 1938, *5*, 89–102.

Lenneberg, E. H. Color naming, color recognition, color discrimination: a re-appraisal. *Perceptual and Motor Skills*, 1961, *12*, 375–382.

Lenneberg, E. H., & Roberts, J. The language of experience, a study in methodology. Memoir 13. *International Journal of American Linguistics*, 1956, *22*.

LeVine, R. A. Cross-cultural study in child psychology. In P. H. Mussen (Ed.), *Carmichael's manual of child psychology*, 1970, Vol. 2, 559–614.

Levi-Strauss, C. *Structural anthropology*. New York: Basic Books, 1963.

Levi-Strauss, C. *The savage mind*. Chicago: The University of Chicago Press, 1966.

Levy-Bruhl, L. *How natives think*. 1910 (in French). Translation. New York: Washington Square Press, 1966.

Levy-Bruhl, L. *Primitive mentality*. 1923 (in French). Translation. Boston: Beacon Press, 1966.

Luria, A. R. *Higher cortical functions in man*. New York: Basic Books, 1966.

Luria, A. R. Towards the problem of the historical nature of psychological processes. *International Journal of Psychology*, 1971, *6*, 259–272.

Maier, N. R. F. Reasoning in white rats. *Comparative Psychological Monographs*, 1929 (9).

Marx, K., & Engels, F. *The German ideology*. 1846. Reprint. New York: International Publishers, 1970.

Mead, M. *Continuities in cultural evolution*. New Haven: Yale University Press, 1964.

Miller, G. A. Linguistic communication as a biological process. Herbert Spencer Lecture, Oxford University, Nov. 13, 1970.

Miller, R. J. Cross-cultural research in the perception of pictorial materials. *Psychological Bulletin*, in press.

Moely, B. E., Olson, F. A., Halwes, T. G., & Flavell, J. H. Production deficiency in young children's clustered recall. *Developmental Psychology*, 1969, *1*, 26–34.

Morgan, L. H. *Ancient society*. 1877. Reprint. Cleveland: The World Publishing Co., 1963.

Mundy-Castle, A. C. Pictorial depth perception in Ghanaian children. *International Joural of Psychology*, 1966, *1*, 289–300.

Nadel, S. F. Experiments in culture psychology. *Africa*, 1937, *10*, 421–435.

Olson, D. R. *Cognitive development: the child's acquisition of diagonality*. New York: Academic Press, 1970.

Osgood, C. E. Language universals and psycholinguistics. In J. H. Greenberg, *Universals of language*. Cambridge: The M.I.T. Press, 1963, 299–322.

Osgood, C. E. Semantic differential technique in the comparative study of cultures. *American Anthropologist*, 1964, *66*, 171–200.

Osgood, C. E. The cross-cultural generality of visual-verbal synesthetic tendencies. *Behavioral Science*, 1960, *5*, 146–169.

Piaget, J. *The language and thought of the child*. New York: Harcourt Brace, 1926.

Piaget, J. *Necessité et signification des recherches comparatives en psychologie genetique*. *International Journal of Psychology*, 1966, *1*, 3–13. Translatd by Catherine Dasen with the assistance of Dr. H. Sinclair, J. W. Berry, and P. R. Dasen.

Piaget, J. Piaget's theory. In P. H. Mussen (Ed.), *Carmichael's manual of child psychology*. Vol. 2. New York: Wiley, 1970, 703–732.

Piaget, J. Intellectual evolution from adolescence to adulthood. *Human Development*, 1972, *15*, 1–12.

Piaget, J. & Inhelder, B. *The psychology of the child*. New York: Basic Books, 1969.

Pollack, R. H., & Silvar, S. D. Magnitude of the Muller-Lyer illusion in children as a function of the pigmentations of the Fundus oculi. *Psychonomic Science*, 1967, *8*, 83–84.

Pollack, R. H. Müller-Lyer illusion: effect of age, lightness contrast and hue. *Science*, 1970, *170*, 93–94.

Price-Williams, D. R. Abstract and concrete modes of classification in a primitive society. *Britsh Journal of Educatonal Psychology*, 1962, *32*, 50–61.

Price-Williams, D. R., Gordon, W., & Ramirez, M. Skill and conservation: a study of pottery-making children. *Developmental Psychology*, 1969, *1*, 769.

Rapaport, D. *Emotions and memory*. New York: International University Press, 1950.

Rivers, W. H. R. Introduction and vision. In A. C. Haddon (Ed.), *Reports of the Cambridge anthropological expedition to the Torres Straits*. Vol. II, Pt. 1. Cambridge, England: The University Press, 1901.

Scribner, S. Logics: one or two? Presented at symposium on logical processes. Eastern Psychological Association, Washington, D.C., May 1973.

Scribner, S. Organization and recall in a West African traditional society. Unpublished.

Segall, M. H., Campbell, D. T., & Herskovitz, M. J. *The influence of culture on visual perception.* Chicago: Bobbs-Merrill, 1966.

Serpell, R. Cultural differences in attention preference for color over form. *International Journal of Psychology,* 1969, *4,* 1–8.

Sharp, D. W. Discrimiation learning and discrimination transfer as related to dimension dominance and dimensional variation among Kpelle children. Unpublished doctoral dissertation, University of California, Irvine, 1971.

Sharp, D. W., & Cole, M. Patterns of responding in the word associations of West African children. *Child Development,* 1972, *43* (1), 55–65.

Smith, J., & Miller, G. A. *The genesis of language.* Cambridge, Mass.: M.I.T. Press, 1966.

Spencer, H. *First principles.* 1862. Reprint. New York: The DeWitt Revolving Fund, Inc., 1958.

Spencer, H. *The principles of psychology.* Vol. I. New York: D. Appleton & Co., 1887 (third edition).

Spencer, H. *The principles of sociology.* Vol. I. New York: D. Appleton & Co., 1888 (third edition).

Stefflre, V., Vales, V., & Morley, L. Language and cognition in Yucatan: A cross-cultural replication. *Journal of Personality and Social Psychology,* 1966, *4,* 112–115.

Suchman, R. G. Color-form preference, discriminative accuracy and learning of deaf and hearing children. *Child Development,* 1966, *37,* 439–451 (a).

Suchman, R. G. Cultural differences in children's color and form preferences. *Journal of Social Psychology,* 1966, *70,* 3–10 (b).

Suchman, R. G., & Trabasso, T. Color and form preference in young children. *Journal of Experimental Child Psychology,* 1966, *3,* 177–187.

Topoff, H. R. The oldest race in history. In E. Tobach (Ed.), *Four horsemen of the apocalypse.* New York: Behavorial Publications, in press.

Turnbull, C. *The forest people: a study of pygmies of the Congo.* New York: Simon & Schuster, 1961.

Tylor, E. B. *Researches into the early history of mankind and the development of civilization.* 1865. Edited reprint. Chicago: University of Chicago Press, 1964.

Tylor, E. B. *Primitive culture.* Vol. 1, 1871. Reprint. London: J. Murray, 1929.

Wallace, A. F. C. Culture and cognition. *Science,* 1962, *135,* 351–357.

Wallace, A. F. C. *Culture and personality.* New York: Random House, 1970 (second edition).

Wang, H. S. Y. Codability and recognition memory for colors. Presented at Eastern Psychological Association Convention, Boston, 1972.

Werner, H. The concept of development from a comparative and organismic point of view. In D. B. Harris (Ed.), *The concept of development.* Minneapolis: University of Minnesota Press, 1957.

Werner, H. *Comparative psychology of mental development.* 1948. Reprint. New York: Science Editions, 1961.

Werner, H., & Kaplan, B. The developmental approach to cognition: its relevance to the psychological interpretation of anthropological and ethnolinguistic data. *American Anthropologist,* 1956, *58,* 866–880.

Wertheimer, M. *Productive thinking.* New York: Harper & Brothers, 1959 (enlarged edition).

Whorf, B. L. *Language, thought and reality.* Boston: M.I.T. Press; New York: Wiley, 1956.

Witkin, H. A. A cognitive-style approach to cross-cultural research. *International Journal of Psychology,* 1967, *2,* 233–250.

Wober, M. Adapting Witkin's field independence theory to accommodate new information from Africa. *British Journal of Psychology,* 1967, *58,* 29–38.

Further Readings

We have selected books and articles for this reading list that we think will be useful as general-purpose reference works or that deal with issues emphasized in the text. The reading list is not intended to be exhaustive, since, after completion of the manuscript, a number of important studies have been published that shed new light on research questions we have discussed. To keep up with current research, we recommend you consult such periodicals as *International Journal of Psychology, Journal of Cross-Cultural Psychology, International Journal of Cognition, Journal of Social Psychology, Child Development, Developmental Psychology, Journal of Experimental Psychology*. In *References*, you will find other periodicals listed that publish papers in specialized areas such as perception and language and, from time to time, carry reports of cross-cultural research.

Cross-Cultural Psychology: Books and General Reviews

Al-Issa, I. and Dennis, W. *Cross-cultural studies of behavior*. New York: Holt, Rinehart & Winston, 1970.

Berry, J. W. and Dasen, P. R. *Culture and cognition: readings in cross-cultural psychology*. New York: Harper & Row, 1973.

Dawson, J. L. M. *Culture and perception*. New York: Wiley, 1973.

Glick, J. Cognitive development in cross-cultural perspective. In F. Horowitz *et al. Review of child development research* Vol. 4, Chicago: University of Chicago Press. In press.

Kaplan, B. (Ed.). *Studying personality cross-culturally*. New York: Row, Peterson, 1961.

LeVine, R. Cross-cultural study in child psychology. In P. Mussen (Ed.). *Carmichael's manual of child psychology*. Vol. II New York: John Wiley & Sons, 1970.

Lloyd, B. B. *Perception and cognition: A cross-cultural perspective*. Harmondsworth: Penguin Books, 1972.

Price-Williams, D. R. (Ed.). *Cross-cultural studies*. Harmondsworth: Penguin Books, Ltd., 1969.

Taifel, H. Social and cultural factors in perception. In G. Lindzey and E. Aronson (Eds.). *The Handbook of social psychology*. Vol. 3., Reading, Mass., Addison-Wesley, 1969.

Triandis, H. C. Psychology and culture. *Annual Review of Psychology*, 1973, *24*, pp. 355–378.

Vernon, P. E. *Intelligence and cultural environment.* London: Methuen, 1969.

Contemporary Anthropological Approaches to Cognition

Thought Systems in other Cultures

Diamond, S. (Ed.). *Primitive views of the world.* (First published as chapters in *Culture in History: Essays in Honor of Paul Radin*), New York: Columbia University Press, 1960.

Gladwin, T. *East is a big bird.* Cambridge: Harvard University Press, 1970.

Goody, J. R. (Ed.) *Literacy in traditional societies.* Cambridge: Cambridge University Press, 1968.

Goody, J. R. and Watt, I. The consequences of literacy. *Comparative studies in sociology and history,* 1962, *5,* 304–345.

Gluckman, M. The logic of African science and witchcraft. *Rhodes-Livingstone Journal,* 1944, *1,* 61.

Horton, R. African traditional thought and Western science. Part I. *Africa,* 1967, *37,* 70–71. Part II, 1967, *37,* 155–187.

Horton, R. and Finney, R. *Modes of thought.* London: Faber & Faber, 1973.

Learning and Cognitive Processes

Bateson, G. Social planning and the concept of 'deutero-learning'. In G. Bateson, *Steps to an ecology of mind.* New York: Ballantine Books, 1972.

Cazden, C. B. and John, V. P. Learning in American Indian children. In M. L. Wax, S. Diamond, and F. O. Gearing, *Anthropological perspectives on education.* New York: Basic Books, 1971, 252–272.

Frake, C. O. The ethnographic study of cognitive systems. In T. Gladwin and W. C. Sturtevant (Eds.). *Anthropology and human behavior.* Washington: Anthropological Society of Washington, 1962, 72–85.

French, D. The relationship of anthropology to studies in perception and cognition. In S. Koch (Ed.). *Psychology: A study of a science.* Vol. 6. New York: McGraw-Hill, 388–428.

Hoijer, H. *Language in culture.* Chicago: University of Chicago Press, 1954.

Leacock, E. At play in African villages. *Play.* A Natural History Magazine Special Supplement. New York: American Museum of Natural History, Dec. 1971, 60–65.

Mead, M. *Continuities in cultural evolution.* New Haven: Yale University Press, 1964.

Murray, A. V. *The school in the bush.* London: Frank Cass, 1967.

Raum, O. F. *Chaga childhood.* London: Oxford University Press, 1940.

Read, M. *Children of their fathers.* London: Methuen, 1959.

Romney, A. K. and D'Andrade, R. G. Transcultural studies in cognition. *American Anthropologist,* 1964, Part II, 66.

Tyler, S. A. *Cogitive anthropology.* New York: Holt, Rinehart & Winston, 1969.

Whiting, J. M. *Becoming a Kwoma.* New Haven: Yale University Press, 1941.

Problems of Method and Interpretation in Cross-Cultural Research

Barker, R. G. and Barker, L. S. Behavior units for the comparative study of cultures. In B. Kaplan (Ed.). *Studying personality cross-culturally.* New York: Row, Peterson, 1961.

Berry, J. W. On cross-cultural comparability. *International Journal of Psychology,* 1969, *4*, 119–128.

Brislin, R. W. Back translation for cross-cultural research. *Journal of cross-cultural psychology,* 1970, *1*, 185–216.

Brislin, R. W., Lonner, W. J., and Throndike, R. M. *Cross-cultural research methods.* New York: John Wiley & Sons, 1973.

Campbell, D. T. Distinguishing differences of perception from failures of communication in cross-cultural studies. In F.C.S. Northrop and H. H. Livingston (Ed.). *Cross-cultural understanding: epistemology in anthropology.* New York: Harper and Row, 1964.

Cole, M. Toward an ethnographic psychology. Paper delivered at the Conference on the Interface between Culture and Learning, Honolulu, February, 1973.

Cole, M. and Bruner, J. S. Cultural differences and inferences about psychological processes. *American Psychologist,* 1971, *26*, 867–876.

Cryns, A. G. J. African intelligence: a critical survey of cross-cultural intelligence research in Africa south of the Sahara. *Journal of Social Psychology,* 1962, *57*, 283–301.

Doob, L. W. Psychological research in nonliterate societies. *American Psychologist,* 1957, *12*, 756–758.

Frijda, N. H. and Jahoda, G. On the scope and methods of cross-cultural research. *International Journal of Psychology,* 1966. Reprinted in D. R. Price-Williams (Ed.). *Cross-cultural studies.* Harmondsworth: Penguin Books, Ltd., 1969.

Goodnow, J. J. Problems in research in culture and thought. In D. Elkind and J. Flavell (Eds.). *Studies in cognitive development*. New York: Oxford University Press, 1969.

Naroll, A. and Cohen, R. (Eds.). *A handbook of method in cultural anthropology*. Garden City, New York: The Natural History Press, 1970.

Pike, K. L. Emic and etic standpoints for the description of behavior. In K. L. Pike. *Language in relation to a unified theory of the structure of human behavior. Part I*. (Preliminary edition). Glendale: Summer Institute of Linguistics, 1954.

Strodbeck, F. Considerations of meta-method in cross-cultural studies. In D. R. Price-Williams (Ed.). *Cross-cultural studies*. Harmondsworth: Penguin Books, Ltd., 1969.

Whiting, J. W. M. The cross-cultural method. In G. Lindzey (Ed.). *The handbook of social psychology*. Vol. I Reading, Mass.: Addison-Wesley, 1954.

Whiting, J. W. M. Methods and problems in cross-cultural research. In G. Lindzey, and E. Aronson (Eds.). *Handbook of Social Psychology*. Vol. 2 (2nd ed.). Reading, Mass.: Addison-Wesley, 1968, pp. 693–728.

Wober, M. Distinguishing centri-cultural from cross-cultural tests and research. *Perceptual and Motor Skills*, 1969, 28, 488.

Credits

Excerpts from *The Measurement of Mental Functions in Primitive Groups* by Florence L. Goodenough reproduced by permission of the American Anthropological Association from the *American Anthropologist*, Vol. 38, No. 1, 1936.

Figure 4-1, courtesy of Harrison Owen.

Figure 4-2, courtesy of The Metropolitan Museum of Art, Rogers Fund 1906.

Figure 4-3 was reprinted from the *International Journal of Psychology*, 1966, Vol. 1, p. 291, by permission of the International Union of Psychological Science and Dunod Editeur, Paris.

Figure 4-5 was reprinted from the *International Journal of Psychology*, 1968, Vol. 3, p. 150, by permission of the International Union of Psychological Science and Dunod Editeur, Paris.

Figure 4-7 was reproduced by permission of the American Psychological Association from *Psychological Monograph*, 1951, Vol. 65, p. 6.

Figure 5-1 was reproduced from *Studies in Cognitive Growth*, by Jerome Bruner, Rose Olver and Patricia Greenfield, 1966, John Wiley & Sons, Inc., p. 285.

Figure 5-2 was reprinted from *Studies in Cognitive Growth*, by Jerome Bruner, Rose Olver and Patricia Greenfield, 1966, John Wiley & Sons, Inc., p. 290.

Figure 5-4 was reprinted from *The Cultural Context of Learning and Thinking*, by Michael Cole, John Gay, Joseph A. Glick and Donald W. Sharp, copyright © 1971 by Basic Books, Inc., Publishers, New York, N.Y.

Figure 5-5 was reprinted from *The Cultural Context of Learning and Thinking* by Michael Cole, John Gay, Joseph A. Glick and Donald W. Sharp, copyright © 1971 by Basic Books, Inc., Publishers, New York, N.Y.

Figure 7-2 was reprinted from *Studies in Cognitive Growth* by Jerome Bruner, Rose Olver, and Patricia Greenfield, 1966, John Wiley & Sons, Inc., p. 233.

author index

subject index